The Lady in Blue

The Memoirs of
India's First Lady Air Marshal

The Lady in Blue

The Memoirs of
India's First Lady Air Marshal

Air Marshal (Dr) Padma Bandopadhyay (Retd)
PVSM, AVSM, VSM

ZORBA BOOKS

ZORBA BOOKS

Published in India by Zorba Books, 2017

Website: www.zorbabooks.com
Email: info@zorbabooks.com

Copyright © Padma Bandopadhyay

ISBN Print Book - 978-93-86407-96-2
ISBN eBook - 978-93-86407-97-9

Although the author and publisher have made every effort to ensure the accuracy and completeness of information contained in this book, we assume no responsibility for errors, inaccuracies, omissions, or any inconsistencies herein. Any slights on people, places, or organizations are unintentional.

Zorba Books Pvt. Ltd.(opc)
Gurgaon, INDIA

Printed at Repro Knowledgecast Limited, Thane

To my late husband
Professor Wing Commander
(Dr) Satinath Bandopadhyay Vishisht Seva Medal

AND

To all young women with stars in their eyes,
"to touch the sky with glory".

Acknowledgement

My heartfelt and sincere thanks to my late husband, Professor Wing Commander (Dr) Satinath Bandopadhyay Vishisht Seva Medal who encouraged me to write my Autobiography. He wrote the first chapter of the same to wake up this slumbering elephant. The short stories are a just a snapshot of my life.

Our sons, Dr. Amiya and Er. Ajit and our grandsons Arjun, Madhav and Sanjay constantly encouraged me and shared their brilliant ideas from time to time. They helped me to correct, edit and select a title for the book and the cover design.

My sincere thanks to Indian Air Force, Army Medical Corps, and DIPAS, DRDO for giving me myriad opportunities, which form the base of these stories.

Sincere thanks to Zorba Books who ensured that I moved forward and did not stop till the book was completed. Their valuable guidance at every step of book creation was a boon.

I thank my friends who helped me fill in many gaps in the narration and were very appreciative of my efforts.

Last but not the least, I would like to thank the many nameless, faceless persons in the narration, without whom I could not have woven the stories.

Contents

Life at Tirupati

All of us have heard of the renowned and the wealthiest temple at Tirupati of Lord Venkateshwara or Balaji and of the famous Laddus of Tirupati. Many of us have visited this temple at Tirumala and the town below at Tirupati. As a toddler, I woke up listening to *Venkateshwara Suprabhatam* by Bharat Ratna MS Subbalakshmi, gently wafting through the temple town of Tirupati.

I was born in a pious South Indian, middle-class family rooted deeply in its values, customs, and traditions. I was named Padmavathy, after the name of the Goddess and consort of Lord Venkateswara, Padmavathy. My pet name was Paddu.

At Tirupati

Prasadams at the temple

I remember the p*rasadams* (eatables distributed to all the devotees after offering it to God). My maternal grandpa's house was in the lane called a*graharam* (where brahmins lived) right in front of Lord Govindaraja temple at Tirupati. Every day, around noon, The Lord was offered *prasadam*, and the *prasadam* would be distributed to all devotees who were present at the temple. The prasadams were c*hakkarai pongal* (sweet khichdi), *ven pongal* (khichdi), *laddus,* etc. As soon as the temple bells tolled, we kids made a beeline and were the first to reach the sanctum sanctorum to receive the *prasadam*. We used to spread both the palms together, and the *pujari* (priest) would give us the *prasadams* in a small plantain leaf enough to fill our hands. The *prasadam* was our lunch. Similarly, at night, the *prasadam* was distributed after the evening puja. This time, it was not that elaborate as in the afternoon but very sumptuous indeed for a child. As a small child, I almost grew up on the prasadams of Lord Govindaraja.

Dinner at home

When we visited Tirupati on vacation, the dinner was not served on plates or banana leaves. My grandmother would mix *sambar* (lentil curry) and *rasam* (lentil soup) with rice. All her grandchildren would sit around her. She would make small balls and feed us along with all the Ramayana and Mahabharata stories and their interpretation which are still vividly printed in my memory. The last item was always curd and rice. She was very affectionate. We could not touch her or the food before it was served to God. Otherwise, the poor lady would have a bath and cook all over again. What patience! She was unlettered. I must confess that this dinner was in addition to the *prasadams* which we had at the temple.

What about you as a grandmother? I am also a proud grandmother of three grandsons. Well, I do help my grandsons in their studies. The children are busy with their computer games and have no time to listen to my stories. To be honest, my story bank is limited; and I feel I need time to enjoy my TV serials too. The present generation is crazy for fast food and computer games.

Hairdressing

Please do not confuse with modern day beauty salons and hairdressers. My grandmother was very fond of me; I was, after all, the first granddaughter of the family. I used to have thick beautiful, black hair which is considered a sign of beauty in India. Every day, she would decorate my hair with different sweet-smelling flowers, and I enjoyed the special attention bestowed on me. My cousin sister happened to be there on one such occasion. She did not have any hair as she had just had her *mundana* (a ceremony where the head is shaved off and the hair is offered to God.). She was very jealous of the special attention being bestowed on me, by my grandmother. Sibling rivalry. One day she insisted her hair also to be decorated with flowers. My grandmother jokingly asked her to put a nail on her head so that she could decorate her hair with flowers. She took a hammer and was about to put a nail in her head. Thank God, we caught her in time and avoided any mishap. Lesson learnt- 'Be very careful when you talk to small kids. They do not know what they are doing and may land up harming themselves'.

Military Hotel

I went on a tour of Tirupati, with my elder brother as a tour guide. He was showing off his Telugu speaking skill, the local language. His initial schooling was at Tirupati. We felt hungry, and he took me to a 'military' hotel. In South India, military is a euphemism for hotels serving non-vegetarian food.

Though I have completed four decades of service in the Armed Forces, I still wonder why the term military was coined for a hotel where non-vegetarian food was served. We had lovely *idlis* and *sambhar* along with fresh coconut *chutney* to our heart's content. I now wonder whether the sambar contained the essence of meat broth! When we returned home, my maternal grandmother called us over for breakfast. We were already full, with *idli-sambhar* that we had eaten at the military hotel. We were young and uninitiated in the art of telling lies; we blurted out our adventure. My grandma was very upset, she took us outside the house and poured *kodams* (pitcher) of water, mixed with few drops of holy Ganges water on both of us, to purify us. She gave us a change of clothing, we changed into the new set of clothing. All this was done outside the house on the street. Only then, we could enter the house. Can you imagine such a scene today?

Pain in the neck for shopkeepers

At Tirupati, there were many small shopkeepers, selling their wares right in the verandah of their houses. They used to sell photos of Lord Venkateshwara, Lord Govindaraja, Goddess Alamelu Manga and Goddess Padmavathy and other Gods and Goddesses. Along with this, they would sell wooden toys, and most importantly wigs made up of artificial hair. But they would pass it off as hair which the devotees have donated to the Lord. They would sell these items at a steep price and thus swindle the devotees who came from all over India. The devotees were keen to take home a souvenir. Whenever a customer would approach the shop, we would get together and call out the real price of the item and shout that they were being cheated. If the customer left the shop because of our shouting, the shopkeeper would chase us and shoo us away from the shop. After a few minutes, we would re-assemble with even more children in our battalion.

Collecting Water

Those were the days of steam engines. Tirupati had water shortage. When we would hear the shrill whistle of the steam engine, women of all age groups would run to the railway station, nearby. The driver knew us all and we would fill up two *kodams* of hot water each from the train. There was no RO plant, and this was our drinking water for the day.

My youngest grandson in the USA plays with all types of trains. Trains are his favourite toys. When I see him with the trains, I remember my days at Tirupati, collecting water from the steam engine.

Rangoli

Today, my grandsons ask me why I get up so early in the morning. Early morning, we had to clean the front porch of the house and sprinkle a mixture of cow dung and water, we do so till date. After the cleaning, we would decorate the area with *rangoli* (patterns made from rice powder). The idea of this exercise was to help in feeding the birds, ants and other small insects who set out early in the morning to search for food. If we were late, we would find no birds as they would have flown away. This was a sort of beautification with the motive of feeding birds and other living beings (*daan*). This habit of 'early to rise' has seeped into my system. Whatever may be the weather and wherever I may be, I wake up early in the morning, but no *Rangoli*.

At Tirupati, Lord Govindaraja was taken out in a procession in the evenings. So, we used to make a fresh *rangoli* for the evening and offered prayers when the procession stopped at our portico. There was a healthy competition in making the *rangolis*. In the process, I learned a lot of new patterns. Now, I do not remember them as I hardly make *rangolis* now.

Monkey menace

In any temple town in India, you will see two things, one beggar and the other our ancestors, the monkey. My grandmother had made some *papads* and spread them on the terrace for drying. She asked me to stay there with a stick to drive away the monkeys. Till then, I had never seen a monkey, as I lived in Madras and Delhi. Sitting on the terrace as a guard for the *papads,* I was lost in my dreams. Suddenly, I realized I was surrounded by monkeys. As instructed by my grandma, I tried to shoo them with my stick following the dictum, 'offence is the best form of defence'. The monkeys must have sensed that I am a child and feared them. They started coming closer to me and bared their teeth as if they would bite me. I was very scared. Down below, all men including my father were gathered and were discussing something near a well. I could not shout because of fear. I saw my father and jumped towards him. Thank God, he caught me, although it was unexpected. Right next to him was the well. I could have fallen into the well. I was saved. Till date, I am mortally scared of monkeys and the scene flashes before my eyes, whenever I see a monkey.

At Tirumala

Many of you will prefer going to Tirumala by air as it saves time. Some may prefer a direct train to Tirupati and then hire a taxi or a luxury car and reach Tirumala. A group of people can hire a luxury bus to reach Tirumala. *Aam Admi* (the common man) travels by state bus from Tirupati to Tirumala. Various modes of transportation are available, directly proportional to your wallet and time availability. Can you imagine trekking from Tirupati to Tirumala with your family and friends? That is how we would reach Tirumala from Tirupati when I was a kid. On the way, we would cook food and sleep under a star-studded sky. It would take about two days of trekking to reach Tirumala.

Gali Gopuram

When you trek towards Tirumala, you pass through a *gopuram*. There are 1000 steps, to reach the *gopuram*. It is called *gali* (wind) *gopuram* as the wind howls here. I think we were coming down from Tirumala to Tirupati and reached *gali gopuram*. After a brief rest, we set out towards Tirupati. In my enthusiasm to reach home fast, I was jumping two steps at a time, and I missed a step and tumbled down like Jill, in the nursery rhyme. My father did some acrobatic manoeuvre (he is a good tennis player) and caught me after about ten steps of tumbling. I had bruises all over, and I was in terrible pain. With Lord Balaji's grace, nothing catastrophic happened.

Buying tickets

We used to have *darshan* without the serpentine queues we see today. I feel the queues are growing longer by the day because of country's population explosion resulting in more number of devotees and devotees wanting everything fast. There are a lot of options available to today's visitor. Many types of *sevas* like *Suprabhata seva, Tomala Seva, Sahasranama Archana* are available at various times of the day. At each of the *seva*, Lord is dressed differently and exquisitely so you can lose yourself in his *darshan*. One must buy a ticket for each *seva*. Though I am not in favour of expensive tickets but to streamline the crowd and to cater to a visitor pressed for time, this may be required. Last time, I visited the temple was about three years back, I did not trek but hired a taxi. I found a special queue for the senior citizens where fingerprinting and photos were taken before letting us inside. Good security and modern techniques are being used now to control the crowd. Everything has changed, from trekking to aeroplanes, from standing in a small queue for *darshan* to a quick special *darshan* and from big laddus to small laddus. There is a queue for everything. It is good that people wait for their turn and do not bulldoze their way. This place makes me feel happy and spiritual.

I spent memorable days of my childhood at Tirupati. I still visit Tirupati often, and old memories come flooding back. Life at Tirupati has changed a lot.

Family Tree

Every family has a story to tell. I would like to share my family's stories, its roots and branches, that have shaped the person I have become. I will talk about my paternal and maternal grandparents and aunts and uncle who directly or indirectly, in good or bad ways, left a lasting imprint on my psyche.

My father hails from the village of Unjalur, a well-known place. This pastoral haven is beautiful with emerald green paddy fields and the sacred river Cauvery flowing through it. A broad-gauge rail line connects the village.

I remember these minute details but in reality; I do not want to remember any part of it at all. Why? You may ask. In my service documents, my father had filled in Unjalur as my hometown, and I was stuck with this 'fact' until the end of my service career. But, I have spent precisely ten days in Unjalur in my entire life. You may think, 'but she is from Unjalur. What is she cribbing about?' Every time you are awarded the President's Medal, the state government (the state specified in one's service joining documents) may reward you by giving land or honorarium. Tamil Nadu, which is where Unjalur is, gives a measly amount as honorarium when compared to Punjab/Haryana/Delhi and other states. If my father had written Delhi, where I spent my entire childhood and completed my schooling and college, I would have benefited more. The answer lies in the fact that no one, including me, was aware of such situations arising in the future. While on a practical level, it would have been better to have had Delhi as my hometown, I am proud to be from the famous village of Unjalur.

This brings us to why the village is renowned. Most of you would not have heard of the famous singer, KP Sundarambal. In Tamil Nadu, people revere her. She sang Tamil devotional songs in praise of 'Lord *Murugan*'. The initial 'K' in her name stands for Kodumudi, which is a large village next to Unjalur. Unjalur, a neighbour of Kodumudi, basked in the reflected glory of KP Sundarambal!

I remember meeting a young lady Flying Officer at a social function. She came running up to meet me and said she was happy to meet and converse with me. I asked her the reason. Her reply stunned me! She said, she was from Unjalur and informed me that the whole village was dying to meet me. I was amazed as I had always thought that nobody would recognize me. Then and there, I decided to visit our village soon.

Gluttony as ancestry!

I vividly remember a story my father narrated to me about my great-great-grandfather, Sri Venkatrama Iyar. This poor brahmin, well versed in the Vedas, was apparently a glutton. The local ruler decided to send some special sweets as a gift to his king, his mentor. Special sweets - *appams* (made of rice, *jaggery* and coconut) were readied. My great-grandfather was ordered to take the sweets to the king. The sweets were packed in a huge cylindrical vessel and covered. He carried the vessel on his head and walked. When he was tired, he sat down under a tree to rest. The aroma of the *appams* was wafting around him, and he could not resist the temptation of tasting the sweet. He reasoned that the king would not get to know about one missing *appam*. So, he decided to wolf down just one of the delectable sweets. In the same vein, at every place he stopped for rest, he consumed a few, and by the end of the day's journey, the vessel was empty. When the king received the empty vessel, he was furious. He asked my great grandfather to explain, and he blurted out the truth. The king found it hard to believe that such a thin man could wolf down all the *appams* in one day.

He ordered my great grandfather to eat rice (the same amount of rice that was used to make the *appams*) along with *sambhar, rasam* and curd, etc. in front of him and run. The king told him that whatever area he covered while running would be his. If he could not eat either the food or run or both, he would be beheaded at once. My ancestor ate all the food set in front of him; once he was done, he started running. He strategized brilliantly. He ran in such a way that he covered villages that lay alongside a large lake. True to his word, the king gifted him all the villages along with the lake. Tamil Nadu suffers from droughts very often; hence every water source is a boon.

The *appams* were made from *aaru padi* (approximately 12 kgs) of rice. So, we came to be known as 'Aaru Padi Venkatrama Iyar's' descendants. I belong to a very renowned gourmand family having its origins in gluttony!

I hardly have any memories of my paternal grandmother. I visited Unjalur when I was about ten years old. She was very sick and bedridden. She recognised all her grand-children including me, spoke softly to all of us and blessed us all. She passed away peacefully soon after. That was my first and only interaction with her.

Memories of my paternal grandfather

Even today, my grandfather, Shri Venkatrama Iyar evokes fear in me. My elder brother was the only one who could stand up to him. The first time I saw him was at Unjalur when my grandmother was on her deathbed. *Thatha* (grandfather) came to stay with us in Delhi after her death. My elder uncle was staying close by too, so my grandfather would shuttle between the two houses. He had a lot of money but was quite miserly; he wouldn't even give us half *anna* (coin) to buy toffee. You had to earn money from him. And what were we supposed to do to earn the money? To get two *annas* from him, the competition could be to drink 20 glasses of water or eat 60 *idlis* in one sitting. My elder brother would never let go of a chance to get two *annas* from our *thatha* and would always win these competitions. Despite my brother completing the tasks assigned to him, *thatha* would not part with his two *annas* but would initiate another challenge. It was great fun watching grandfather and grandson. Grudgingly, *Thatha* used to give my brother the two *annas*.

Every time I think of *thatha* and my brother, I remember this nursery rhyme in Hindi where the grandchildren ask for a *paisa* to have ice-cream, and the grandmother refuses. Then the children sing," Jaldi *se ek paise de, Tu kanjoosi chod de* ".

My paternal grandfather was educated, had great regard for education and expected every child to be a wizard in mathematics. He had worked under the British Government and was drawing a pension of ₹6/- per month. At the age of eighty-five, all his teeth were intact, and he had near-perfect vision. He never wore dentures or spectacles. He had a booming voice and could never speak softly. When he would call out to my father and uncle, he could be heard clearly across a half kilometre radius! He had long hair which he wore in the traditional Brahmin style. Daily, he would massage his hair with coconut oil or curd or *mehndi*. He took care of himself and his good health, even in his eighties, was a testament to that.

His one duty, I vividly remember, was to sit in the outside veranda. My elder brother had a lot of friends who would call him out to play. But, first, they had to pass the firewall test of my grandfather. The first question he would ask them would be - what is your father's name? He did not comprehend the name and surname concept that is prevalent in North India. So, the next question would be about their job and emoluments. If the answer was satisfactory, the next and final question would range from simple arithmetic and Vedic mathematics to the Pythagoras theorem and set theory. The poor children would run for their life! My brother used to sneak out of the house and play with them. The kids hated his interview and especially mathematics questions.

With me, he would insist that I listen to only classical Carnatic music. In those days, a Murphy transistor was our proud possession. If he ever found us listening to Hindi songs, he would confiscate the transistor and complain to our father. As a result, when I joined medical college, I proudly announced that I could sing during one of the ragging sessions. When they asked me to sing, I sang a classical Carnatic song. Later, I became the joker of the batch. Later, I picked up not only Hindi but also Bengali songs quite easily. Basic knowledge of classical music helps you pick up most genres of music.

Towards the end of his stay in Delhi, my grandfather banged himself against a chair and developed a non-healing *ulcer* (wound). He was taken to Willingdon Hospital (now known as Dr Ram Monohar Lohia Hospital). He was diagnosed with Diabetes and advised on diet and treatment. When my father insisted on following the advice of the doctor, my grandfather gave my father a stern lecture on how ignorant doctors were and left for Unjalur at once. He was about ninety years old then. He never followed any diet schedule and never took the prescribed medicines. He died a natural death at his ancestral home about two years after leaving Delhi.

Shri NV Baskara Iyar, my maternal grandfather

I have vague memories of Shri NV Baskara Iyar, my maternal grandfather. He was a short, dark man. He was always dressed in a *vesti* smeared with all the VIBGYOR colours. He was very quick-tempered and always carried snuff in the folds of his *vesti*. My grandfather owned a hotel in Tirupati. At the peak of his career, he had a roaring business. He kept the money in *kodams* at home. Maybe there were no banks nearby at that time, or no one believed in banks in those days.

My grandfather was an excellent host and treated guests with reverence when they visited him in Tirupati. My grandmother was always in the kitchen, cleaning, chopping, cooking and serving at least 50 people daily. Guests were gods in their house *"Atithi Devo Bhava"*. If by any chance, meals were delayed, my grandfather used to throw the *aruvamanai* (cutting board) at my poor grandmother. When we used to visit them during holidays, he would make special *dosai* for my elder brother. I was never given even a morsel of this special *dosai*. If ever I asked for some, he would shoot me away, asking me to go home and eat. He was very short-tempered and did not believe in gender equality.

My maternal grandfather was uneducated, but he was a self-made man. He earned pots and pots of money but died a pauper. Many times I feel sad when I think of him. He deserved a much better life, especially in his old age. The number of people he fed, the number of people he educated are all legendary. He helped a lot in looking after my mother during her protracted illness. But he passed away quietly, an unsung hero.

My beautiful Patti

My maternal grandmother or *Patti* was a complete contrast to my grandfather in looks. Called Lakshmi, she was the most beautiful woman I have ever met in my life. Very fair, small built, always dressed in pure silk, nine-yard sarees, I remember her as always busy in the kitchen. If she touched anything, she would wash and wipe her hands immediately. She would generously feed one and all and was the last to partake of food. Once she'd eaten, she would immediately start cleaning vessels, chopping vegetables for dinner and grinding for next day's breakfast. Nobody was allowed into the kitchen other than the women of the household and that too only after they had bathed and finished their *puja*.

She was very affectionate. We hardly had direct contact with her as she was always busy in the kitchen. We could not touch her or the food before it was served to God. Otherwise, the poor lady would be forced to have another bath and cook all over again. What patience she had. She tolerated my grandfather's anger with forbearance; she never uttered a word even though many a time she was hurt badly. She was unlettered but her life skills, which she imparted to us, were phenomenal.

Once, she came to Delhi to help us when my mother was in the hospital. It was winter, I recall, and on the very auspicious *Vaikunta Ekadasi* day, which is sometime around the end of

December/early January, my elder brother played a trick on her. After her bath, while she was busy cooking, he went and touched her. She went and had a bath again and restarted the cooking process. My elder brother repeated the same trick again and again. Her entire collection of nine-yard sarees were washed that day! Finally, she ran out of sarees to wear after her bath and so no food was cooked. The net result was that we went hungry for two days. Why for two days? No food was cooked for two days, as she could not change into a fresh saree after her bath. Why did she have no saree? Since it was winter, the sun was weak, and her sarees were not drying. There were no washing machines in those days. My brother got a good walloping.

My grandmother's name, as I mentioned earlier, was *Lakshmi*. She looked like Goddess *Lakshmi*, lived a royal life and was *Lakshmi* to the whole family since we were all prosperous so long she lived. She died a queen. My grandfather also passed away soon after that.

Chitti (Smt Parvatambal)

Chitti was my grandmother. She was the wife of my grandfather's younger brother, Shri Rama Iyer and was my mother's paternal aunt. *Chitti's* story was pathetic. I am writing about it to impress on all how difficult it is to bring up an adopted child at a late age.

My grandfather's brother was a very big zamindar, and *Chitti* had at least eight to ten young girls helping her out in the various household duties. My mental picture of *Chitti* is that of a queen. She was always well dressed in *kanjeevaram* silk sarees with gold and diamond jewellery adorning her.

She adopted a boy when they were quite old, against the wishes of my grandfather. To have a son is the prime goal in life in a Hindu family. The adopted son was thoroughly spoiled and turned out to be a useless brat. He never even passed his class X. In the meantime, *Chitti's* husband passed away due to old age. Thankfully, he did not live to see the miserable life *Chitti* had to suffer thereafter.

The adopted son fell into bad company as there was no one to check him, and became a drunkard. He used to beat his mother; he sold all her jewels initially and later the land too to finance his drinking. During this time, he was married and had two sons. His wife was educated and was a teacher in the local village school. Facing this hopeless situation, she kept herself busy with her profession and educated her boys. Her sons are well settled today.

However, *Chitti* and her adopted son had to fend for themselves. Over time, they reached a stage when there was no money for food. At this point, I intervened and sent them cash every month so that they could at least eat curd and rice. On one occasion, I visited *Chitti*. I wish I had not seen her. She was bent and was walking on all fours. Since she did not know how to use a gas stove, she was cooking rice for her son and herself on an *angiti* (iron stove) She was ninety-two years old at that time. The profligate son by now had lost his eyesight and was shouting away due to the ill effects of alcohol. What a pitiable sight. I sobbed at her plight. Was it necessary? I do not know. Hindus believe in past *karma*. Maybe that was to blame. I prayed for her early departure from this world. She passed away sometime later.

It is to be seriously debated whether she needed to adopt a child at that late stage of her life. Did she get anything worthwhile from this son? When his wife did not take care of him, this old lady was cooking for him. A person who lived like a queen died a pauper with no one to care for her. What a tragic tale?

Memories of my first film

My aunt, my mother's only sister, was educated up to class 8 and was my grandfather's pet. One incident involving her is still etched in my memory. Once, my aunt and her husband (my mother's cousin) had come to visit my mother in Madras. They decided to go for a movie and insisted on taking me along with them. I had never gone for a movie till then. My mother was very reluctant to let me go. After much persuasion, my mother finally permitted them to take me along. I still remember the name of the film. In Tamil, it was titled, *Vazhkai* and had 'Vyjayanthimala' in the female lead role. However, I was made to stand near the door while they went in. For the entire duration of the film, I was standing outside near the entrance gate. I still remember one of the songs: *'collegepadithum payanillai, car ootta terindum payanillai.'* I cried all through the film.

I still wonder why they did that to me – take me for the film and then leave me all alone at the entrance. Now that I am in the evening of my own life, I try to speculate on the reason. I guess my aunt genuinely wanted me to enjoy an outing. Maybe her husband was opposed to the idea. And in those days, the wife had no choice except to obey her husband's wishes. They must have come to a compromise – I got to go on an outing, but I could not go in with them. After they left, I narrated the incident to my mother. She cried inconsolably. My aunt passed away on the very day I got married. Because of the sad news of her passing away, my wedding was tinged with sadness. Irrespective of the film incident, I think we both shared some sort of a special bond.

My paternal uncle (Periappa)

I had three elder paternal uncles. The eldest lived in our village, Unjalur. I hardly remember him except that he had long hair, tied in the traditional style and had huge ruby ear tops. He always wore a *vesti*, either with a towel slung over his shoulder or a shirt. I had interacted with him on very few occasions.

My other two uncles were brilliant and highly educated. The elder one was also a famous astrologer. The President of India had honoured him as one of the best *Jyothishi*. He never charged for his astrological predictions. He had three daughters and one son. The son passed away following a fall from the rooftop. Periappa's eldest daughter, Kannamma is my best friend; we have been close right from childhood till date. Both my uncles lived long and crossed ninety years of age. I remember my astrologer uncle remarking that he was ninety-one not out. Nevertheless, this wonderful soul passed away when he was around ninety-two years old.

His wife, my aunt, was very fond of me. Losing her only son was a huge shock to her, and she never got over it. She used to cook delicious food and snacks and would always give me some to eat. I used to save whatever she gave me and would share it with my brothers. The act of sharing enhanced the taste of the snacks. I still remember her fondly and cherish her affection towards me.

My journey from this traditional Tamil background to a Bengali household and later to international brotherhood was a journey punctuated with several learning curves - some easy and some difficult. During this journey, I understood the true meaning of *vasudaiva kutumbakam* - the world is one family.

Mother and Me at Madras

It is quite common that once a person enters the later phases of life, looking back over the journey, thus far becomes an exercise in awe and gratitude. Life is a rollercoaster ride of the most uplifting peaks of successes and the most painful pits of failures - a medley of new births and great losses. Yet, the passage of time brings perspective and wisdom with it. Today, my children have grown, and my grandchildren are thriving. I can truly reflect on the many hardships I had to surmount as well as the several mentors and guides who helped me along the path. I do not miss childhood, but I miss the pleasure I took in small things, even as greater things crumbled. I could not walk away from things or people or moments that hurt, but I took joy in the things that made me happy.

If someone had told me during my childhood that someday I'd be accepted into the Indian Air Force, or be awarded the Vishisht Seva Medal (VSM) for my participation in the Indo-Pakistan War, I would not have believed them. If, as a young girl, I had been told I'd go on to become the first woman Aviation Medicine specialist or be the first Indian woman to conduct scientific research at the North Pole, I would have laughed in disbelief. Perhaps most shocking to me would have been hearing that someday I'd become the first woman Air Marshal of the Indian Air Force.

I believe that my faith and value system played a major role in my successes. From childhood, I strongly felt that anyone could achieve their dreams, provided they worked hard at it. I never had any problems with prayers or rituals, however weird they were. My surroundings and environment brought about many positive changes in me and helped develop many habits that I nurture even today. I never trusted in rituals blindly, but questioned them and tried to find answers with my limited knowledge. I believed that every human being was the same no matter their caste, religion, status or nationality. I strongly believed that a man or woman, boy or girl could become whatever they dreamt of becoming with hard work and determination, not just because of the families and circumstance they were born into.

It was through focus and determination that I could come so far, but many people helped me along the way. Over the years, while I struck many obstacles and nearly gave up hope, friends and teachers, family members and superiors within the armed forces as well as strangers and close confidants stepped up to offer their help and support. In addition to the kind souls who assisted me during my journey, I had many amazing people to watch and learn from while growing up. My mother Srimati Alamelu Swaminathan was one such role model.

It was after the delivery of my younger brother, when I was just three years old, that our mother fell ill. What began as a low-grade fever and severe backache was left unaddressed for months. She couldn't be treated by anyone other than a female Brahmin doctor, and finding one proved to be extremely difficult. On top of that, our mother's symptoms were initially thought to be the normal side effects of childbirth. With the development of a *purulent* (pus) discharge, my grandparents realized that it was a severe situation. When a doctor was finally called in to see her, it was suspected she had tuberculosis (TB), a deadly epidemic sweeping India in those days. My mother was taken to the TB Sanitorium at Madanapalli near Tirupati in the present-day Andhra Pradesh where she was diagnosed with bone (spine) tuberculosis. The following year, she was transferred to Madras for better medical treatment.

At that time, elders did not know whether she would recover or not. And even if she did recover, no one knew how long the recovery process would take and will there be a disability? I followed her to Madras, where I spent the next one year tending to her as best as I could. The daily household tasks often seemed impossible given my young age. My mother was immobile, forced to lie flat on her back on a hard, wooden bed. Household chores like cleaning, cooking, and feeding her were all up to my four-year-old self.

I still remember the house where we lived in Madras. It was in a central area, and there was a big music hall right at the end of the road. The house belonged to one Mr. Pillai. He had two sons and a daughter and several cows and buffalos. The younger son was affected by polio and could not walk. The lady of the house was very fond of me. She used to feed me whenever the rice got burnt in our home. Initially, I used to tell my mother about it, and she would ask me not to eat in their house. However, I was a little glutton! Whenever I was hungry, which happened to be quite often, this loving lady fed me. I stopped telling my mother. Why did my mother put these restrictions on me? It was because they belonged to a different caste, which I did not understand then. Even today, I don't subscribe to outdated views like this.

My school days

My school in Madras was the best educational institution I have seen till date. It was a small school with few teachers, but the teachers were exceptional and very friendly. We were taught only two subjects - Tamil and arithmetic. Without paper or pencil, we'd trace shapes in the sand, and wipe them away once we had learned them. There was no homework, no truckload of books and notebooks to be carried. The sand was our slate; there were no fancy laptops or tablets. The teacher used to feed us our lunch and then sing lullabies. Post lunch, we slept for about two hours; once we woke up, it was time to go home. Please do not underestimate the school because of its unconventional teaching methods. Whatever we learnt then, is still fresh in my memory. I can still recite my tables, not only up to 16 x 16 but also ½; ¼; 1/8 and 1/16. Because those were the days of rupees, annas and paise. What made the school exceptional was that they did not make us learn everything by rote. The teachers took pains to make learning interesting and took keen interest in our learning. We never had to go for tuition to enhance our learning.

In India, most children begin school around the age of two. It is such a tedious process because kids must mug up so many things and vomit them out in front of the interview board to get admission in a decent nursery school. Parents are not spared either; they too are interviewed. I believe that the best school education system in the world is in Finland where children start going to school at the age of seven. There is no homework and no examinations up to around middle school. Compared to what children in India face today regarding education, we had a much smoother sailing. A recent study concluded that children in classes IX to XII are under tremendous stress. I pity the children in present-day India.

Household chores

I remember struggling to fetch fresh water for household chores. To get potable water, I'd struggle to pump the hand pump to fill my *kodam*, then clumsily balance it around my waist and haul it up a huge flight of stairs. By the time, I arrived at our quarters, the vessel would be half-full, and I would be soaking wet. However, I welcomed being soaked since the heat in Madras was searing and you would be bone dry in a jiffy.

Cooking was another ordeal. I'd prepare all the meals for us on a kerosene pump stove. I wasn't a great cook and all I could venture to prepare, was rice. While lying flat on her back on the hard-wooden cot, my mother would instruct me on how to light the stove and cook the rice. Often the rice turned out to be a *kanji* (porridge); or half-burnt or improperly cooked. Not surprising! Daily, a hawker woman would visit with a basket of assorted herbs, leafy vegetables, curd and curry leaves for seasoning. I looked forward to her visits eagerly because she provided the accompaniments of curd and lemon pickle for my poorly-cooked rice. My maternal grandmother would visit us often, at least once in 15 days, and stay on for two to three days. When she was around, she would cook us delicious meals. Glutton that I was, I enjoyed the food. Before leaving, she would make many dry *chutneys* which we could mix and eat with rice or add to the curd rice. We survived our entire stay in Madras on these flavours.

My elder brother's visits

My elder brother would occasionally accompany grandmother to visit us in Madras. My mother, but naturally, loved his visits as she could at least get to see her elder son. However, for me, rather than being joyous and peaceful, his visits were very stressful. For starters, there was a language barrier between him and me. He was raised in Tirupati, under the care of my maternal uncle and spoke Telugu. I spoke only Tamil. My mother spoke both languages and could communicate with both of us. However, she was unable to control my brother's truant behaviour. Because she was bedridden and immobile, she could only scold him, once he'd returned home after his escapades.

During one such traumatic visit, he nearly lost his life in the Bay of Bengal. He did not know how to swim so I do not know why he decided to wade into the sea. He began to drown and providentially, was spotted by some fishermen nearby in an unconscious state. My memories of the event are limited as I was very young. The fishermen revived him and carried him along the streets shouting so that the boy could be identified. Fortunately, they bumped into distant relatives of ours who identified my brother and rushed him to the hospital. My mother, helpless, cried in her bed. When news arrived that he had survived, she continued to cry in relief. S Kalyan, my younger brother, was the final addition at that time to our childhood trio. Born three years after me, he was raised in our native village in Tamil Nadu.

Return to Delhi

Our father was based in Delhi and worked year-round. With little time off, he was unable to visit each of his three children spread across three different locations. To support his family, he'd send money. All this changed when I was around five years old, and our father decided to reunite the family. At this point, I had been living with my mother in Madras for one year. Motivated in part by Delhi's advanced medical facilities, and partly by the desire to live together as a family, he collected our still sickly mother and all the children, and moved us to north India.

My mother was admitted to Safdarjang Hospital immediately after reaching Delhi. Being a devout and orthodox Brahmin, she ate rice and curd provided by the hospital. She feared that lentil curry and vegetables could be mixed with non-vegetarian ingredients. She was admitted to the general ward, so there were no guarantees that the food would be totally vegetarian. So, for 24 hours a day, seven days a week, 365 days each year, she lived on rice and curd. She continued fighting for her life for several more years in the hospital.

My mother's strength and courage

Looking back, I can only attribute my mother's survival to her strong motivation to live. I saw for myself that if the desire and drive are there, a person can pull through every hardship and overcome any obstacle.

Watching my mother's will to live, and her determination to survive, had a profound effect on me as a young girl. No matter how painful or difficult her situation was, she refused to give up hope. No matter how hopeless she felt, she greeted me every morning with a loving smile. I was exposed to her strength and courage every day. It would be several more years before my path towards medical college or the air force would begin to take shape, but spending those early years by my mother's side instilled in me the belief that if a person is willing to work hard and never give up, they can accomplish many great things.

My Parents

Whatever you are or will be in the world is because of your parents. It was through focus and determination that I could come so far, but my parents were my first support and help. Over the years, when I hit many obstacles and nearly gave up all hope, my parents gave me the courage to continue. They are my primary role models.

My father:

His childhood

My grandfather resigned his government job (he was working under the British) for the sake of his children's education. My father, Sri Venkatraman Swaminathan is the youngest of four brothers. He has just completed 102 years; is a simple, pious, hardworking and spiritual senior citizen. He blindly followed the diktats of my grandfather when he was young. When he grew up, he obeyed his elder brothers. My father was obedient to a fault and never asked any questions.

Admission to school

The story of how my father was admitted to school is an interesting one. My grandfather told his elder son to get him admitted and told him his date of birth verbally. In those days, there were no birth certificates as almost all deliveries took place at home. Both the brothers reached the school. The elder brother forgot the date of birth his father had told him. Once my grandfather began his *puja*, no one was supposed to disturb him. He was almost like Lord Shiva and would get angry with anyone who disturbed him. Since my grandfather was engrossed in his *puja*, the brothers knew they could not approach him. They decided to be innovative and devised a new method. They wrote out different dates on three small pieces of paper and asked the

Pujari (priest) of the village temple to choose one. The slip of paper the *pujari* selected became my father's official date of birth. Thus, his official date of birth as per documents is about eight months later than his actual birthday; the correct date of birth is April 15, 1916. He gained eight months of service though he left service earlier. The flip side was that he had to wait for eight more months to become 100 years officially.

His breakfast and tiffin

What was his breakfast and *tiffin* in those days? Leftover rice post-dinner, soaked overnight in water in an earthen pot. Curd was always available at home. Each household had at least two or three cows or buffalos for their daily needs. So, breakfast was simple - rice, curd and salt served on a banana leaf. The same simple fare was packed for school; this time too in a banana leaf that was slightly wilted so that it was more pliable for packing. Unlike in modern times, mothers in those days did not ask their children what they wanted for breakfast or *tiffin*; kids just ate what they were given! It was a life of simplicity.

The school uniform was a small *vesti* up to primary school. My father and his brothers had to swim across the river Cauvery to reach their school. They would dry themselves with the towel and wrap it around like a *lungi* in school. Every child wore a similar outfit, so it was no big deal. There were no girls in the school. By the time my father and his brothers started going to school, they were all expert swimmers. They learnt swimming not from swimming coaches but by clutching onto a log of wood or a pumpkin or riding on a buffalo. It must have been very exciting to be amidst nature all the time and learn so much from it.

My father did not carry kilos of books stuffed in a huge bag. Today's kids carry such heavy loads to school – I wonder whether this heavyweight really makes one intelligent or into a heavyweight champion! These heavy school bags can be detrimental to health – it leads to backaches and spinal deformities at a later age. All school work was completed in school and there was *no homework* in the primary section. How simple life was!

My parents' wedding

My father was nineteen years old and my mother just nine years old when they were married. In those days, marriage alliances would take place between boys and girls of nearby villages. The best advertisement was word of mouth. All marriages were arranged. The elders in the family would visit the girl's house and the marriage would be settled if the horoscopes matched. The little girls had no inkling about what marriage was. They were so young that it seemed like a doll's marriage. Dowry was not a very big issue then. Dowry in Tamil is called s*idhanam,* a twisted way of pronouncing *sreedhan* – the gifts and gold brought by the daughter-in-law.

My mother's illness

When my mother fell sick, my father was very young and could have married again. But, he opted to look after all of us, including his ailing wife. He sold off whatever he had and imported medicines for my mother from the UK. He was lucky to have been working under the British, who helped him in procuring the medicines. My mother survived because of timely medication.

My father shifted all of us to Delhi. My mother was immediately admitted to Safdarjung hospital for further treatment. In the early days in Delhi, our father used to cook for all three of us, after returning from office late at night. He would make *sambhar* and rice. The top portion of the *sambhar* was *rasam* and the thick portion at the bottom was the *sambhar*. In those days, there were no pressure cookers or cooking gas. It used to take ages to cook on the stove (*angiti*), especially in winter, with *lakdi koyla* (soft coke) and *pathar koila* (steam coke).

My father used to return home late at night after almost 12 hours of gruelling work and no refreshments in between. Being a staunch Brahmin, he wouldn't eat or drink anywhere other than home. Most days, we children used to sleep off owing to hunger and because of the cold during the winters. It was his usual practice to jump the wall of the house if we were asleep. Once, during his adventure of jumping the wall, *Appa* (my father) was caught by a policeman and interrogated. Of course, he was set free, but this resulted in all of us getting beaten with a cane by *Appa*. Many a time, my elder brother was beaten black and blue. We were terribly scared of him and did not like him.

Service career

My father came to Delhi and joined government service in the Finance Ministry and rose to become Under Secretary in the Ministry of Law. He retired at the age of 58, after serving for nearly 33 years. His superior wanted to give him an extension for two more years as he was very hard working, sincere and, most importantly, a man of high integrity. However, my father refused the extension. He did not have pots of money, but he was utterly contented. His youngest son had at that time been admitted to engineering college. He had also just bought a house in Madras for which he had to pay the equated monthly instalments (EMIs). He managed all the expenses with his pension and enjoyed his retirement by playing tennis.

There is an interesting incident that occurred during his career. During the time of the British Raj, my father served under a British Minister who was very strict. The summer capital of India in those days was Shimla. The day before the minister moved to Shimla, he had handed over an important file to my father for safe custody. This file was essential for a meeting. On the scheduled date of the meeting at Shimla, he asked my father for the file. My father searched high and low but could not find it. As bad luck would have it, his *chaprasi* had kept the file safely in Delhi rather than putting it in the trunk marked 'SECRET', which had gone to Shimla with the minister. Since the minister was getting late for his meeting, he lost his temper. My father was very apologetic and tried to explain what had happened. The minister was red-faced and interrupted by saying, "Your services are terminated with immediate effect," and postponed the meeting by a day. My father hurried out of the office and reached the Delhi office in record time, God knows how! He caught hold of the *chaprasi*, grabbed the file and rushed back to Shimla the next day, where the meeting was in progress. The minister was so happy that he called him in, looked at his pale, unshaven visage and his shabby outfit and said, "You are reinstated with double promotion." Throughout his service spanning about four decades, his schedule was to reach office one hour in advance and to leave the office, one hour after his boss left.

His love for tennis

Appa was a good tennis player and has always been passionate about the sport. When my mother was sick, he had to perform all the household duties in addition to his official duties. He still found time to squeeze in some tennis. His biggest luxury purchase was a pair of tennis shoes for ₹1. Even when the sole was torn, he would re-sole it with rubber and play for some more time. Even today, when he can hardly see, he wakes up at odd hours to watch tennis matches being broadcasted from different parts of the world. I am sure that at this moment, he is watching his favourite sport being played somewhere in this world!

My father and I

As Matthew Jacobson said, "Behind every young child who believes in himself/herself is a parent who believed first." As a little girl, I was extremely scared of him. I remember how he cut my beautiful long tresses and gave me a crew-cut, as he could not groom my hair. I hated him for this. All that changed after my class XI results, when I saw how serious he was about my education.

He ran from pillar to post to admit me in pre-medical because I had finally decided to become a doctor after passing class XI in the Humanities stream. When I was worried about learning science, he would give me pep talks. He would always inspire me by assuring me that I could scale any height, however difficult it may be. He allowed me to join the Armed Forces Medical

College and continue in the Armed Forces after completing medical college. I repaid him with honour and respect. He was my guest of honour at the Investiture Parades and had the opportunity to interact with the President and Prime Minister of India and other dignitaries during those functions. He is very proud of me.

When I decided to get married, *appa* consented to my marrying a Bengali Brahmin despite his conservative background. This was owing to my father's unflinching support towards me and his faith and trust in me. After we got married, he gave me only one piece of advice: "Never complain against or crib about their family as it is your family now; try to do your best for your family and never come back crying to us." My father loved and respected Satinath Bandopadhyay, his only son-in-law. He was very proud of him for never letting his daughter down. My husband always encouraged me and supported me in all my academic and adventurous activities. My father could not have imagined a better, more caring, sharing and loving life partner for his daughter.

At DSSC

While at Defence Services Staff College (DSSC) at Wellington, Ooty, India, *appa* looked after me, my children and the house and, of course, enjoyed his tennis. His tennis was appreciated by one and all. He used to beat both Indian and foreign young student officers. One day, my course-mate, a German officer, walked into our house to check what special diet I was feeding my father! When he saw the rice, lentil with vegetables and curd, his jaw dropped in utter surprise. Believe it or not, there is a terracotta mug in my house which is at least 46 years old. It was never I but my father, who used to pack during our moves from one place to another. My father taught me how to take care of all the household items.

I remember another funny incident. The plastic cover over the toilet commode had a hairline crack. While handing over the house when I was posted out of DSSC, I was asked to pay for the replacement of commode. I was well versed in this game. If I had paid, the commode would never have been replaced and every other officer would have been fleeced. My father put some adhesive and sat on the seat cover for about two hours. The hairline crack disappeared, and no one had to pay.

Our sons' weddings

Our sons also followed in our footsteps. They decided on their life partners and conveyed their decisions to us. There were several arguments and counter-arguments. It was my father who finally sealed the decision with his approval. Both his grandsons and their wives dote on him. Despite his orthodox upbringing, he maintained that if the children wanted to lead their lives with their chosen life partners, why should we create hurdles. If we, as elders, continued with our age-old views, he reasoned that the children would run away. We would end up losing our children. I wish people would heed this advice and help young couples to lead happy married lives instead of killing them in the name of caste, creed, religion, etc.

Even at this ripe old age, my father is active. Till date, he boils milk for the morning coffee, washes his own clothes and waters some of the flowering plants. The flowers are offered to the Almighty. He keeps praying, meditates for the good of this universe and for everyone. He is a true *Karmayogi*. When I was growing up, he was my first role model. He might have scared us when we were young, but as we matured, we began to appreciate the sacrifices he made for the family.

My Mother

Srimati Alamelu Swaminathan

I do not know much about my mother's childhood. They were four siblings. Like me, she was the second child; she had an elder brother and two younger siblings - a sister and a brother. She never went to school but learnt Tamil at home. She was well versed in all the household jobs, which was the most important

QR for a girl child. She was married off at the age of nine and came to Delhi when she was around sixteen years. My mother was diagnosed with bone (spine) TB after the delivery of my younger brother. She was about twenty-one years old at that time.

When we moved to Delhi, my mother was admitted to Safdarjung Hospital. She continued to be an inpatient for around five to six years. Despite the frugal food intake, she survived. My mother used to tell us that her motivation to fight the disease and live came from her children. She wanted to take care of the three of us. We used to visit her once a week with homemade filter coffee. It was like a picnic for us. Maybe the seeds of desire to become a doctor were sown in my mind from those days of visiting my mother in the hospital. When *amma* was in the hospital, I used to feel that life was not fair, but I carried on. I realized later that however good or bad a situation is, it will change.

When Amma came home

After almost a decade of hospitalisation and being bedridden, my mother had forgotten how to walk. She relearnt walking by dragging a chair. What a royal life we all led after my mother's return from the hospital. I felt like a princess. My mother used up all her nine-yard Kancheepuram silk sarees to make dresses for me along with matching blouses. My friends were green with envy as the girl who till then used to look uncouth and shabby had turned into a princess overnight. My mother took over all the household chores. I just had to go to school prettily decked up. *amma* would sweep, swab and cook delicious food for all of us. We did not have to lift even a little finger. She massaged my hair with coconut oil every day and washed off the oil with homemade shampoo once a week. You must listen to how my hair was dried after shampoo? She would place burning umbers and put some incense, '*sambirani*' to add fragrance to hair post a nice oil bath. This was cover with an upturned basket and my wet hair was spread over the top of the basket. The hair used to dry gradually and used to smell nice. My mother learnt knitting during her years of being bedridden in the hospital. She knitted beautiful sweaters for all of us. She saved every *paise* for our wellbeing. She prayed fervently for her children and her prayers always protected us from the evil eye.

During our examinations, she would stay awake and feed us with coffee and hot snacks. In return, we would slyly read story books instead of textbooks.

Learning Hindi

My mother did not know Hindi when she arrived in Delhi at the age of sixteen. She learnt Hindi from a Tamil magazine, *Kalki*. But her Hindi was more *shudh* than mine.

There is an incident that is fixed in my memory. My father was very fond of animals and our house was a mini zoo. We grew up with a minimum of two to three dogs, one or two deer and a few cats. My father used to bring home discarded pedigreed pups and feed them with milk from a bottle attached to a nipple. When they were a little bigger and opened their eyes, his next task would be to toilet train them. My father's friends would then adopt these pups. He also used to make medicines for dogs with local herbs. One day, he made some medicine for his friend's dog. He told my mother to hand over the medicines to his friend when he came home to collect the same. He told my mother that the medicine was for their dog. When the gentleman arrived, my mother first shut the door (reminiscent of *purdah*), then announced, *Kutha ka dawai uta lo, aur tum pi lo* (please take medicine for the dog, and you drink it). He was confused at first but later realized that it was her Hindi that had caused the confusion. We all had a hearty laugh when he narrated the incident to us.

I remember that *amma* could not count money. My father used to put the correct amount in different envelopes for the vegetable vendor, milkman, the helper and so on. He would write their names in Tamil and hand over the envelopes to her, which she would then distribute. That is how the bills were paid in our household!

Orthodox upbringing

My mother was a very orthodox *tambrahm* (Tamil Brahmin). I had grown up by then and had attained menarche. My youngest brother was sixteen years younger than me. At times, both my mother and I would get our menstrual periods at the same time. My poor brother would keep crying and finally doze off because of hunger. Neither she would enter the kitchen, nor allow me to enter, as it was not allowed. She followed all the customs and rituals of the letter very sincerely. Later, despite her orthodoxy, she accepted my house which stocked non-vegetarian food items in the fridge. She knew very well that I cooked non-vegetarian food, but she also knew that I remained a pure vegetarian.

Last days

On the morning of that fateful day, my mother served the morning coffee in a tumbler and *dabara* (a kind of saucer) to my father and then went into coma. She never recovered and passed away after two days in coma. She was a severe hypertensive and was on medication. She completed all her duties before she left this physical world to be at the lotus feet of God Almighty.

My mother served as an inspiration for me. Watching her will to live, and seeing her determination to survive, had a profound effect on me as a young girl. No matter how painful or difficult her situation was, she refused to give up hope. She greeted me every morning with a loving smile. I was exposed to her strength and courage every day. It would be several more years before my path towards Medical College or the Air Force would begin to take shape, but spending those early years by my mother's side instilled in me the belief that if a person is willing to work hard and never give up, they can accomplish many great things. I admire my mother for all her hard work, for taking care of us and showering us with so much love and affection.

I learnt from my father to believe in God Almighty and hard work. No work is too small or too big. He taught me not to waste even a second and instilled in me many more life skills which till date keep me in good stead.

Parents who are loving and caring are the first step on the ladder for a happy child and a great human being later in life. When children grow up, we must respect them. If they require help in any form, be it financial, emotional or physical, we must be ready. Many youngsters forget their past and feel reluctant to recognise their parents if they are not well off. Without the support and blessings of parents, no child will ever evolve into a good, successful human being.

Both father and mother are very essential for a child to be brought up correctly. I was lucky to have wonderful parents with both my father and mother by my side.

Transformation in Premedical

"Embrace each challenge in your life as an opportunity for self-transformation."

— Bernie S. Siegel

It was June 30, 1960, the day my class XI board exams results were declared. I had scored (520/800) marks with Distinction in Mathematics. My father could not believe the good news and waited for any misprints notice in the next day's newspaper. For the first time in my life, I realized that I was intelligent.

However, I was miserable as I could not join any regular college in Delhi University since I was underaged by a few months. Funnily enough, I was admitted to the nearby Usha Tailoring School to learn tailoring and embroidery. I quit the classes after ten days. My biggest regret was the loss of six months prepaid fees.

My dream

I confessed to my father that I wanted to become a doctor. My father trudged in and out of several colleges, meeting professors and principals, fervently trying to get me admitted into a college. Finally, I was admitted for pre-medical at Kirorimal College in Delhi University. I was the first humanities student to change over to the science stream.

The foremost hurdle when I joined pre-medical was my lack of communication skills. No one spoke to me, and I could not talk to others. The second problem was that I could not study late in the evenings at college. I was not permitted to stay back and study in the library as girls were expected to be home before sunset. If you had to stay back for some reason, prior permission from your parents was a must. On those occasions when I did stay back, my elder brother would pick me up from college and accompany me home.

When my elder brother escorted me, he would put me in the first bus and would follow in the next one. I would alight from the bus and wait for him. We would then walk back home together but with 30 feet between us! He was embarrassed to escort his sister... male chauvinism! However, since we would reach home together, my parents were blissfully unaware. There was an unwritten understanding between us, and neither of us told our parents the truth. Those were the unwritten rules which most young girls followed those days. There is a TV serial these days which paints the picture of a mother worried about her growing daughter. The father is happily settled on the couch with his newspaper. The mother is neither able to confront her daughter directly nor leave her to grow up on her own terms. That was my mother's state when I was growing up. After college hours, I had the choice of either cooking dinner or looking after my kid brother. I preferred babysitting and looked after my adorable younger brother.

The third hurdle I faced in college was a lack of even the most basic knowledge in science subjects. Extra coaching was not a possibility, so I had to work extremely hard.

Dressing up and cultural differences

My mother used to oil my hair and tie two plaits with matching ribbons. She would adorn my hair with flowers like *chameli, mogra* and other sweet-smelling varieties. I used to look like Baji's sister in the serial 'Peshwa Bajirao'. While travelling in the bus, other students used to jeer at me, pull out the flowers, sing songs, etc. I figured that wearing flowers in the hair was looked on askance by non-south Indians. I devised a solution. After I left home for college, I would remove the flowers from my hair and put them in my bag. On my return home, the flowers were back in my hair. I used to wear a *lehenga* (long skirt), blouse and the *dawani* (*dupatta*), a typically south Indian attire. My attire led to many sarcastic remarks and catcalls. I changed to sarees, covering myself from top to toe to avoid any confusion. During the first month of my college life, my plaits, ribbons, flowers and finally the *dawani*...all had to change so that I could be accepted as one amongst the others and not be looked upon as a *madrasi*. Nevertheless, I remained a *madrasi* thanks to my looks.

By nature, I never antagonised or opposed elders and their customs. Maybe I was not courageous enough. I always found ways to sort out the issues without hurting the elders' sentiments.

My best friend philosopher and guide, Elizabeth Varghese (now Alvares)

An angel came to my rescue in the form of 'Lizzie' - a smart, self-reliant and very compassionate and helpful friend. Lizzie was my friend, philosopher and guide for about a decade. The tables turned later. When she used to come home on a visit, the sofas were covered with pretty, removable covers. The coffee was served in a ceramic cup and saucer. Normally, we drank coffee in steel tumblers and *dabaras* (saucers). After Cinderella left, the sofa covers were removed, to be washed, and the ceramic cup and saucer were kept in the veranda to be cleaned... and normalcy was restored. I tried reasoning with my mother but to no avail.

Without Lizzie, I would have never completed my premedical course. I communicated in Tamil (which was the language I spoke) and she replied in Malayalam, which I managed to decipher partly. It was a hilarious situation. She taught me to speak English, and in about six months, I could converse well in English. Still, Hindi was a far cry. She helped me to get over the anxieties of adolescence and the superstitions with which I had grown up till then, and helped me in developing life skills.

Today, the front pages of newspapers are splashed with colourful advertisements of lingerie; turn on the TV and you have flashy ads, promoting sanitary napkins. But, in those days, my mother did not know anything about bras. Neither did she wear one, nor did she buy me one. We used to wear a small sleeveless blouse under the blouse. At college, everyone used to laugh and make fun of me. So, my friend Lizzie advised me to buy a bra. Firstly, where was the money to buy and secondly, how would I use the bra? She devised methodologies to overcome both issues.

She took me shopping and bought two bras with whatever money I had saved. Please remember, in those days, there was no pocket money. When I reached college, I would change into the bra, and before returning home I would remove it. Lizzie used to wash the bra at her house. When I picked up some courage, I told my mother that people were making fun of me and I wanted to wear a bra. She promptly asked me to stop college and stay at home. After a few more months, I grew a little bolder (under the tutelage of Lizzie), and I came home wearing a bra. My poor mother almost collapsed. After a lot of scolding, she allowed me to wear a bra with stipulated conditions. One was that I should wash and dry it covered by other clothes like the petticoat or the sarees and it should not be visible because there were growing boys at home. Second, when I went to college, I should wrap my saree around and cover myself fully. I accepted her conditions.

The next change was sanitary napkins. Initially, it was old used cotton sarees which I used, washed and reused. It was a cumbersome affair. Those few days were a real misery. Not because of health reasons but owing to reasons of hygiene. Firstly, I couldn't bathe for three days. Imagine yourself in Delhi during hot summers without a bath. It was terrible. Secondly, you get only leftover food because you could eat only after everyone had eaten. Thirdly, the napkins. All these factors caused enormous stress. Present-day advertisements for sanitary towels are so explicit and daring. When I was growing up, it was a complete contrast. Everything was kept hush-hush as if having periods was a crime. Maybe, these reasons contributed to young girls not taking part in sports and games and excelling in them. This is how I started my small rebellions. Poor *amma* was not aware that her darling daughter was going to be a rebel. My support and my guru in all this was Lizzie.

She used to come home often. I was supposed to drop her back at the bus stop but instead, would walk her home. We would be engrossed in gossip and would reach her home at Dev Nagar, Karol Bagh by climbing a hillock, which is presently Shankar Road.

Lizzie joined Christian Medical College in Ludhiana after her pre-medical. She took quite a long time to pass out of medical college. Not because she was not good in studies but because of her individualistic views on religion, which she was very outspoken about. I met her again after I got married, in Ludhiana, Punjab where we were posted. Suddenly, she decided to go to Germany and we lost contact. She is now back in Bangalore, a tired, old, sick, elderly lady but she still has that spark. I meet her whenever I go to Bangalore and we reminisce about our golden days. Now, I am her friend, philosopher and guide. The roles have been reversed.

In a DTC bus

For all of us (my brothers and I), the time-tested *tiffin* at school/ college was curd and rice, especially in summer. It is very easy to make but awkward to carry in a Delhi Transport Corporation (DTC) bus. Getting into a DTC bus was itself a herculean task. The bus would never stop at the authorised stop: it would either stop 50 meters ahead or short of the stop. Commuters had to run at least 50 meters before they could reach the bus. You were lucky if it halted; most days it would crawl. When the driver spotted old people or ladies trying to get into the bus, they would drive faster to make their life miserable. There was no concept of chivalry; you either had to run and jump into the bus or someone would push you in through the entry/exit gates while someone else would pull you inside. After this hurdle, you would have to stand till you reached your destination, in my case, Maurice Nagar. Now, the curd rice would start dripping and it could drip onto someone's head or clothes. The person would naturally scowl at you. The only positive – thanks to the dripping- invariably I would get a seat!

Curd rice reminds me of a very interesting episode. My dearest friend, Lizzie's father was a retired physics professor from Lahore. He was hoping against hope that he would get a Nobel prize for Physics one day and worked on several mathematical problems. Lizzie asked me to learn physics from her father on holidays. The first day I was merely introduced to him, and we had lunch together. He was very confident that I would pick up physics in no time. The reason was my curd rice; astounding indeed! The next holiday, I landed up at their place to learn physics from uncle. When I entered his room, I couldn't find him anywhere. I called out to him and then I heard his voice. I looked all around and still could not spot him. Uncle's voice guided me to look up. I looked up and found uncle sitting on top of a ladder, writing some equation on the roof and wall. I do not remember whether I was surprised or shocked. Anyway, he taught me physics, and I grasped the subject well. Uncle was convinced beyond doubt that it was all because of curd rice. Alas, uncle did not get a Nobel till he breathed his last.

Dr Mattoo, my Chemistry Professor

I will always cherish the memory of my chemistry professor at KiroriMal College, Dr Mattoo, who taught me the ABCs of chemistry during lunch break without charging any tuition fees. I can never forget that foundation. The teachers at the college did not understand my ignorance, and I did not have the vocabulary to explain anything to them. I was admitted to a section where everyone had passed out in first division, except that they were all science students. Professor Luthra, the senior-most chemistry professor, predicted that I would never pass in chemistry and used to throw me out of the class every day. What I did unknowingly on the very first day, infuriated him. On that first day, he had written a chemical reaction, i.e.: $KMnO_4 + H_2SO_4 \rightarrow K_2SO_4 + MnSO_4 + H_2O + O_2$ and asked the students to balance this chemical equation.

I took it to be a formula, as in algebra, like $(a+b)^2 = a^2 + b^2 + 2ab$ and wrote the same reaction verbatim. He asked me to show him the equation and promptly told me to get out of the class. He thought I was pulling a fast one on him. I could not explain my predicament because of the language barrier. Every day, he turned me out of the class. If I told of my predicament at home, they would have stopped me from going to college, and I would have been married off at the earliest.

My chemistry practical was another explosive experience. As I did not possess a white lab coat for the first few months, I was turned out of the lab. I used to be outside the lab, praying that I would master chemistry. Sometime later, with a lab coat on, I was struggling to bend glass tubes. Other students knew the basics like bending a glass tube. The more the professor scowled at me, the more glass tubes broke into pieces.

I endured my chemistry classes stoically. After almost six months, Professor Mattoo called me to his room and asked me what the problem was. This was the first time someone had enquired about my problems. First, I broke down inconsolably. Afterwards, I blurted out that I had studied English, mathematics, economics, Tamil and Sanskrit and that I did not know anything about chemistry. He was stunned at my outburst. When he got over it, he assured me that he would teach me chemistry during the lunch break. So, I started with 'A' for Argon, 'B' for Boron and at the end of my pre-medical course, I got a distinction in chemistry. Professor Mattoo did not charge even a rupee as tuition fees. Can we find such dedicated teachers like him today, I wonder?

My limited drawing skills

I managed physics with my mathematics knowledge and uncle's teaching. Biology was not a very big issue as everyone was like me. No one had studied Botany and Zoology in the school. We were all in the same boat. In the botany lab, I was the joker. My free-hand drawing skills were the talk of college. I vividly remember the first day. There was a small flowering plant with branches, leaves and flowers in a flower pot. We were asked to draw the same. The freehand drawing was never my cup of tea. I took out my scale, measured the length of the branch, then measured the angle of the flower from the branch and was trying to draw. My botany professor's jaw fell. He would have never imagined anyone drawing a branch and flowers with a scale and protractor. He asked me, "At this rate how will you ever become a doctor?" His statement was very true. In medical college, it was very tough for me to draw the anatomy and histology diagrams. I must have drawn each figure in the Gray's Anatomy book at least 100 times on my slate. At the end of the day, I could manage some figures which were nowhere near the original. I used to label it as schematic promptly. But my registers were done beautifully. My father used to draw all the diagrams for me. I used to carry one register which had good drawings during vacations. My father industriously copied them for me, and I labelled them all and got maximum marks for the registers.

Realising my dreams

The two years of pre-medical passed very quickly. I passed with 58% marks. I also passed the competitive exam of the All India Institute of Medical Sciences, but I could not join because of financial constraints. I did not get admission in Lady Hardinge Medical College (for women only). After the interview with the Vice-Chancellor, Delhi University, I was permitted to join BSc. Thus, I started my graduation, and I was keenly absorbed in scientific enquiries. I was working on the topic of 'Optical Isomerism'. I dreamt of completing MSc in chemistry and then fly out to USA on a scholarship to become a great scientist. The dream of becoming a doctor had almost vanished from my mind. The next year, I joined AFMC, fulfilling both my dreams of becoming a doctor and serving the nation.

This period of self-transformation required significant changes in my personal life. The scared cat's transformation to a ferocious tiger was almost complete. Change is a part of everyone's life, and we must change for the good. If society is static and does not move forward, so many evils would still prevail today. Women would have remained uneducated, and *Sati* and other social evils would have continued. However, one must weigh the pros and cons before taking the final step to change.

Life-Changing Decisions

When you look back on your life, you realize that certain decisions that you took, or did not take, have played an important role in shaping your future life. I am going to recount a few of the twists and turns in my life which shaped me into the person I am today, a lady with many firsts under her belt including being India's first lady Air Marshal.

Quitting tailoring school

With a record of 65% in Humanities, I could have joined any regular college of my choice at Delhi University (only the north campus existed in those days). Alas, I could not join any college, as I was underage by a few months. As mentioned earlier, my father admitted me in a tailoring school as per my mother's wish. On the face of it, nothing was wrong, but my world went topsy-turvy. I was a young teenager, and I felt that all my happiness had been robbed by the 'Usha Tailoring School'. The combination of my lack of knowledge of Hindi and Punjabi, not having seen a sewing machine at home and the tailoring teacher's snide remarks added fuel to the fire and increased my hatred towards tailoring.

The daily ritual we had to follow was to do a certain number of paper cuttings. The measurements in Punjabi sounded like Greek and Latin to me. I did not understand words like *turpai,* which meant hemming. I did not know what a *bobbin* meant as I had never seen a sewing machine. I was also made fun of by the teacher and other students (mostly married ladies). They would mock me saying that even though I was a distinction holder in mathematics, I did not know simple calculations. As a result, the whole class would have a hearty laugh at my foolishness. It was the month of July, hot and humid, and there was a volcano raging within me at my own helplessness, and it was waiting to explode.

I used to fume at my powerlessness. For a young girl, dreaming of the stars and the moon, this was too much humiliation to bear.

On or about the tenth day of this ordeal, one of the most eventful days of my life, this timid stupid girl mustered up her courage, put the paper cuttings on the table, said *namaste* to the teacher and left the tailoring class once and for all. Six months of prepaid fees were lost entirely. Even today, I cannot stitch anything except replacing broken buttons on shirts, hooks in blouses and some hemming.

What followed the tailoring fiasco? Well, I had a very important job – that of looking after my youngest brother who was born on July 4, 1960. I was kept very busy, and it was interesting to spend time with him, but it did not satisfy my hunger for knowledge. My mother could not fathom my misery. My father did not have any idea about science as he and his elder brothers were students of humanities. Nevertheless, my father had the courage to admit me in the college against all odds. What were the odds? A severe financial crunch. No extra coaching was possible for me, with two of my brothers and two cousins studying in school and one new-born brother to look after. But, he believed in me.

Opting for pre-medical

My poor father found out that doing a premedical course was a pre-requisite to be eligible to apply for admission to a medical college. To fulfil my wish, he started making the rounds of various colleges under Delhi University. My father was also made fun of because humanities student was not permitted to pursue pre-medical. A changeover to the science stream was not allowed. Everywhere he went, he was treated with ridicule and met with a standard reply – a capital 'NO'. Nevertheless, he persisted, and finally, his sincere efforts and my prayers paid off, and I was admitted for pre-medical at Kirorimal College, Delhi University. There was a hard condition attached to my admission. Within six months, I had to master physics, chemistry and biology and pass the half-yearly exam at the end of six months. Now, it was my turn to take up the challenge and face the competition. With my hard work and help from Uncle and Professor Mattoo, I cleared the examinations with flying colours. My decision to walk out of the tailoring class took me from being a good tailor (which had never been my goal) to being eligible for becoming a doctor, my long-cherished dream.

After successfully completing pre-medical, I did not get admission to medical college that year. I had scored 58%, which was not good enough for me to get a medical seat at Lady Hardinge Medical College. Lady Hardinge Medical College was for women only, admitting students from all over India. Admissions were as per your pre-medical/equivalent examination's score. As a child, without even understanding what it takes to become a doctor, I had stood at the entrance to Lady Hardinge Medical College practically every day and prayed to become a doctor and help cure my mother. To me, this college was a temple and not just a college. Girls from nearby states, who had secured more marks than me, were admitted.

Then came a whiff of hope for me as a few seats were allotted for government servants' wards. I was on top of the list with my marks and was eagerly waiting for a call letter, but it never came. Then, to my horror, I found out that a student who had scored much lower marks than me had been admitted. When my father questioned this, we were told that a postcard was sent informing us to report to the medical college on a specific date and time. As we had not responded, the seat was offered to the next in merit. However, we never received any such postcard. Perhaps the letter was dropped in the 'dustbin' after it was noted down in the register as 'Sent'. Even today there is too much fraud and forgery in admissions to medical college. It is disgusting, to say the least. The tragedy was that the girl who was admitted instead of me was married six months after joining the medical college and left. I felt cheated by the system. I did not comprehend God Almighty's designs for me at that juncture.

Why did I not try for the All India Institute of Medical Sciences (AIIMS)? Well, I did, and I passed the competitive exam for the institution in the first attempt itself. However, we could not afford the fees, hostel expenses, etc. So, the idea was dropped. My not so good score in pre-medical and financial constraints held me back from joining a medical college.

Interview with the Vice Chancellor

I was wondering what to do next. I applied for Bachelor of Science(BSc) Chemistry with Botany and Zoology. I was denied admission as I had been an Arts (humanities) student up to class XI. The fact that I had earned a distinction in Chemistry was not factored in. This time I did not ask my father to do the rounds of colleges for my admission. In the last two years, I had learned to speak English and had also developed a certain amount of confidence. When my college principal was unable to help me because of the rules, I plucked up the courage (which I rarely did in those days) to seek an appointment with the Vice Chancellor. I explained my position. However, he too insisted that I could not do a graduation course in science since I had not done science in school. I suddenly became very bold and argued with him. I asked him if that was the reason, why had they admitted me in pre-medical? Two years back I had known no science whatsoever; I had struggled hard to learn and do well in science, and in the process, I forgot mathematics, economics, Tamil and Sanskrit. Now that I had some knowledge of science, I told him that I should be admitted to BSc. If I joined an arts subject, I would be a beginner again as I had no recollection of those subjects. He thought over my argument for some time. Maybe he was wondering how this girl had managed to pass science without any background in the subject. It was important for me to remain in the science stream, to fulfil my dream of becoming a doctor. Finally, after a nail-biting wait of 48 hours, the Vice Chancellor permitted me to do graduation in science.

Choosing AFMC

Initially, I was very disappointed at not making it into Lady Hardinge Medical college in the first attempt. The next year,

I appeared for AFMC and passed the written examination. I preferred AFMC as I was fired up to join the Armed Forces after the 1962 Indo-China war. The interview went off very well despite the initial hiccups which were due to my foolishness. I was keen on contributing to the nation's security, and this was the opportunity. AFMC helped me to qualify not only as a doctor but contributed to the holistic development of my personality. After graduation, I joined the IAF. One of the reasons for joining the IAF was the blue uniform. I, contributed to the nation's security as a medical professional and finally reached the top of the hierarchy as Air Marshal, which in turn brought me so many bouquets. My father wholeheartedly supported me. The rest of our relatives and friends were dead against me joining the Armed Forces since they did not view it as a great career prospect. Thanks to my father's support, I plunged headlong into it even though it was a tough decision for a young girl.

My life partner

My husband contributed immensely to my career successes thanks to his unwavering support. Since he too was in the Armed Forces, he understood my job and stood by me. We also shared a happily married life, which too impacted positively on my career.

Posting as AOC, AFCME

Life on the professional front sped along like the Rajdhani Express at times and crawled like a goods train at other times. Finally, after almost 30 years of service, I was cleared by the promotion board for the rank of one-star General, i.e. Brigadier in the Army and Air Commodore in Air Force. You must be wondering why I am bringing the army rank every-time. All the doctors in Armed Forces belong to Army Medical Corps and are seconded to Navy and Air Force. The doctors in these two services have an army number followed by Navy or Air Force personal number. Whenever we are promoted, first the Army rank followed by the equivalent Navy/ Air Force rank will be published. I had to wait another two years before the promotion was announced. The climax was the place of my new posting. The rumour mills were working overtime. The officer who was tipped to take over as Air Officer Commanding (AOC), Air Force Central Medical Establishment (AFCME), was my senior and he had almost completed his tenure in the Delhi area. In the promotion board, three aviation medicine specialists were also cleared for promotion and all three of us were highly suitable for the post.

For the first time in my life, I gathered up courage and sought an appointment with the Chief of Air Staff (CAS). He was out of the country and his staff officer gave me an appointment to meet him two days after he returned. His instructions to me were hilarious. He said, I quote, "You should be in proper uniform. The uniform should be properly ironed. You should have a service haircut (he seemed to have forgotten that I was a lady officer!). You should not be obese and should be within the stipulated weight criteria. You should not wear flashy jewellery (now he remembered that I was a lady officer!)." I just nodded in agreement. Later, I wondered what I should do with my hair. Finally, I decided to sport my usual hairstyle. I never wore jewellery while in uniform, and thankfully, I was not obese. CAS was very particular that IAF personnel should be fit as a fiddle.

On the day of appointment, I reached 15 minutes in advance and saluted the SO. Now he realized that I was a lady and felt a little uncomfortable about his earlier instructions. I had to wait for a while. As soon as the CAS arrived, I was ushered in. I saluted him and stood. He asked me to sit down and I obeyed. For almost five minutes, I could not speak a syllable. My mouth and tongue had become bone dry. I just looked at him. It was the first time in my service career that I had come with a petition. At that time, I just wanted to vanish from there.

He understood my state of acute anxiety. To ease my obvious discomfort, he started enquiring about my husband and children. Once he started speaking to me, I overcame my anxiety and fear and gradually relaxed. Once I calmed down, I put my views on posting of AOC, AFCME.

On the next day, the expected posting order was not announced, and the then DGMS retired. To cut the story short, I was posted to this prestigious unit AFCME as Air Officer Commanding (AOC). This posting changed my career prospects radically. I put in my best all the time. I was awarded the Presidential award - the Ati Vishisht Seva Medal (AVSM) and was cleared for my next rank, Major General (Air Vice Marshal in IAF), two-star General.

Posting as Additional DGAFMS

There came a point when I had to decide whether to continue in the IAF or quit. After the announcements of the promotion, my placement took a long time, almost a month. In higher ranks, you do not wait that long. My Director General Armed Forces Medical Services (DGAFMS) explained that there was no post for me in the Air Force in the rank of Air Vice Marshal and that I should take over as Major General The other senior officers who were in his office also advised me accordingly. After serving in the Indian Air Force (IAF) for nearly 36 years, I had become a thoroughbred Air Force Officer. I submitted that I wanted to continue in the blue uniform (Lady in Blue) only. I even offered to take premature retirement if I could not be accommodated in the Air Force uniform. It was a difficult decision indeed. The DGAFMS understood my passion for the IAF and asked me to wait for some more time, till he could find a post for me where I could serve without changing uniform. Now the ball was in their court, and I waited for my next promotion while functioning in my previous office as AOC, AFCME.

Like a bolt from the blue, I was posted as Additional DGAFMS which is a very coveted and powerful post. It was a difficult but interesting job, and one needed to tactfully deal with the Defence Ministry, where the junior clerks threw their weight around. If they were not pleased with you, your file could vanish for days, months and even years. The file would never see daylight hidden under mounds of other files. You needed a lot of tact to tackle them. Without the ministry's approval, nothing can happen in the Armed Forces. It was a tough job which did not care for your rank or awards or your qualifications. I managed it well I suppose. There were no major goof ups. After this stint of two years, I was cleared and promoted as the first lady Air Marshal and DGMS (Air) in October 2004.

I firmly believe that you must do what you think is right. To do that, you must make tough decisions. For me, these major but tough decisions shaped my professional and personal life and propelled me towards becoming the first lady Air Marshal and head of medical services in the Indian Air Force. Of course, there were many hiccups along the way because of some wrong decisions. However, life is always a learning curve.

The Late Sri Nandlal Banerjee (Babuji)

Babuji, my father-in-law, was a legend. He was highly educated, Master of Science (MSc) in Physics from the reputed Banaras Hindu University. He was very hardworking and exceptionally talented. He could sing, play the flute and cook delicious dishes. He loved to lead a good life but was also a strict disciplinarian.

Calling on AOC

In the Armed Forces, there is a custom of 'calling on the Boss' as soon as you report to a new unit. This was my first posting, and my boss was Group Captain Dilbagh Singh, who later became the Chief of Air Staff and Ambassador after his retirement. As I was a married woman, I was wondering how to call on the boss without my husband. Finally, I decided to call on my boss with my father-in-law, *Shri* Nandlal Banerjee. I do not remember the finer details of the meeting, but I can still picture my boss's awe-struck expression. *Babuji* was holding court in his physics professor style, and my poor boss sat there, listening in silence. In retrospect, it was quite funny! Finally, the 'calling on' came to an end. *Babuji* had enjoyed it and had even downed a couple of drinks; I, however, was on pins and needles. The family was not used to the service way of life. For that matter, even my knowledge of it was zero. Even today, when I recollect that evening, it brings a smile to my face.

Introduction of tea at home

Before my entry into the Banerjee family, they were not habituated to tea or coffee drinking. I was brought up on filter coffee, possibly one of the strongest coffee. Imagine my plight, when there was not even a cup of tea at home. So, I had to take permission to have two cups of tea - one in the morning and one in the evening. With this, the floodgates opened but quietly.

When I would be sipping my cuppa, my *Ma* (mother-in-law) would sneak in quietly and ask me to give her some tea. Initially, I shared my tea with her. Over time, I started to make her a cup of tea and would serve her. Then, my husband too joined the tea party. But *Babuji* never became a member of this club. To compensate for the loss of tea and coffee at home, I used to consume almost 40 cups of tea while looking after patients in the hospital. I got addicted to tea as the locals did not know how to prepare good coffee.

Babuji and his sons

My father-in-law's elder sons were mortally scared of him. I don't know much about my elder brother-in-law as he and his wife were abroad. My husband's only advice to me was to 'do what *Babuji* says'. The third son would not even stand in front of his father. Can you imagine a qualified engineer getting married without even seeing his future bride once? Well, the third son did just that because *Babuji* had arranged the marriage. Till date, he is the most loving, caring brother-in-law. No one dared to question *Babuji* on any matter.

His youngest son was the only one who had the courage to face *Babuji* and talk. He was his pet and my best friend. He was staying with us and preparing for his National Defence Academy (NDA) examinations. I used to teach him Mathematics and Science in English. As he had studied in Hindi medium, it was difficult for him to comprehend. But, he succeeded with his hard work and successfully completed the NDA course. He joined the army and did very well for himself and contributed immensely to the nation.

My youngest brother-in-law used to stand next to me when I cooked non-vegetarian dishes. He would advise me on what *masalas* I should add. If the dish turned out awful, he would run away and if it was good, he would take the credit. He was my biggest support till my husband joined me. I used to enjoy his mischievous comments and learnt a lot from him about our family.

He was very fond of milk and would have a tall glass of milk every morning and evening. If I forgot to give him his glass of milk, or if milk was in short supply because of guests, he would not get his quota of milk. The next day, he would insist on two glasses together to compensate for the previous day. I enjoyed all his pranks.

I was not good at interior decoration. When he came home from NDA on holidays, he would decorate the house for me and order me not to change the arrangements till he returned after six months. And we both obeyed him. He used to keep bragging that his future wife would be smartly dressed, able to drive a car, good at cooking and good in interior design. Finally, his wife was all that he wished for and it was we who selected a bride for him.

Babuji and my parents

Babuji had great respect for my father and addressed him as *Panditji*. They were very good friends. If by any chance my parents landed up at our place and we had non-vegetarian dishes in the refrigerator, onions and garlic at home, these items were promptly thrown out of the house. When they were at home for one or two days, the food was totally vegetarian. We also had separate cooking vessels and serving spoons that had not been used for non-vegetarian cooking. He did not observe all this out of obligation or for show; he genuinely respected them and did not want to hurt their feelings.

Babuji and Asha (me)

My father-in-law renamed me *Asha*, his hope. He was like a father to me. Even though I was the *bahu* who had to adjust, he too had to make a lot of adjustments to accept me as a *bahuma*. My being a doctor in the armed forces was not the preferred qualitative requirement (QR) for a *bahuma*. He called me 'Asha' and expressed hope that I would be his daughter and look after the family. I tried my best to fulfil my promise to him.

Standing outside the house for returning home late

One evening, a few officers, their spouses (who were my friends) and I decided to go and see a movie in Ludhiana and have dinner out and return by 8 pm. Unfortunately, due to a power cut, the movie started at 5 pm instead of 3 pm; as a result, everything got delayed. I enjoyed both the film and the dinner. We came back at around 10 pm. *Babuji* would not open the front door. I stood outside the door; *Babuji* was on the other side of the door but the door was not opened till morning. *Babuji* kept telling me across the closed door that he was responsible for my safety till my husband came on posting and that I should have been more responsible and not come back so late. He believed that I should have skipped the film or the dinner. At that young age, it was a very strict disciplinary action. I learnt my lesson the hard way. A far cry from what happens these days. I was a gazetted officer belonging to the armed forces and a doctor by profession. At that point of time, I was very angry and upset with *Babuji*. Twenty years later, I tried to discipline my niece in a similar way. Of course, she did not give a damn for my discipline. That is the way of life now. But *Babuji* really cared for me. He would cycle down to the hospital with my lunch box if I were stuck there owing to an emergency. He would wait till I attended the emergency, feed me and then go home. His advice: "Eat at the proper time and work hard."

Ludhiana bus trip

Babuji decided to visit Meerut where they had lived before my husband and I got married. For nearly three months they had left their home unattended. Also, he wanted me to visit the Meerut house. I was granted a few days leave and all three of us reached the bus stand with all our stuff safely locked up in a steel trunk as was in vogue those days. *Babuji* was carrying the trunk. The bus arrived. The conductor asked my mother-in-law and me to get in and told *Babuji* to get in after the ladies. Once all the ladies had got in, the bus left. *Babuji* was left behind. He started running frantically behind the bus with the huge steel trunk.

Ma and I were standing near the bus driver. I requested the bus driver to stop the bus, but he would not. The conductor made fun of me in Punjabi, asking what a *madrasi* could do now. His exact words were, "*madrasi kuddi, tussi ki kar loge*". I was wild. I did not know enough Punjabi to give him a fitting reply, but I had understood what he'd said. Not one passenger came out in support of us. I repeatedly requested them to stop but to no avail. Finally, I had to become like 'Ma Kali'; I broke the windshield glass in front of the driver with my briefcase. Then, all hell broke loose, and the bus stopped. My mother-in-law and I got off the bus and joined *Babuji*. We took the next bus. It is common all over India to face similar attitudes from bus drivers, conductors and co-passengers.

Tonga ride

There was no direct train to Meerut from Punjab. We boarded the train at Ludhiana after the bus ride and disembarked at Delhi junction and boarded another train. Thus, our memorable journey brought us to our destination, Meerut. It was about 1 am if I remember correctly. *Ma* and I were checking the luggage and *Babuji* was in the process of hiring a *tonga* (horse carriage). Suddenly, we heard a loud noise and turned towards *Babuji*. He had slapped the *tongawala*, a tall, well-built fellow, right royally as he was asking for a higher fare. I was stunned and at the same time scared at *Babuji's* heroics - a middle-aged man slapping a well-built *tongawala* in the dead of night. He was accompanied by a middle-aged lady, his wife, and a young newly married lady, his daughter-in-law. I could not believe my eyes. *Babuji* was a very short-tempered man but had a heart of gold. It took me time to understand him. Finally, our epic journey ended, and we reached home.

Buying vegetables

I had never bought vegetables before I got married. At Delhi, there was a *sabjiwala* (vegetable vendor) who brought vegetables in a *tonga*; he used to take our orders and deliver the items at home and would collect the money at the end of the month. In my parent's house, we hardly ate potatoes. One day, *Babuji* asked me to buy potatoes from the *mandi* (wholesale vegetable market). I reached the *mandi* in my new second-hand car and asked the *sabjiwala* to give me one kilo of potatoes. From my uncertain behaviour, I am sure he understood that I was a novice in this field. He selected the worst potatoes for me. I came back home without realising that I had rotten stuff. *Babuji* was very angry at my stupidity and shouted his lungs out. I was a hothead at that stage. When I got fed up with his shouting, I retorted by saying that I had passed MBBS with distinction and gold medal and had not done it for buying potatoes. There was pin-drop silence. No one had ever retaliated to *Babuji's* shouting till then.

Scooter accident

My younger brother-in-law and his newly-wed wife came over to our place to celebrate *Durga Puja*. We decided to visit the *puja* celebrations in Ludhiana and have some fun there. We took permission from *Babuji* to be out till 6-7 pm and set course on two scooters. We had a good time but were late in returning. We knew we had to be home by the deadline. To be home on time, my husband was driving at top speed. In those days, we had to cross a railway line at a small station called Mullanpur. There were pebbles, small and big, piled up near the railway track. As we were crossing the railway line, the scooter skidded, and I was thrown off. Luckily, I held onto the footboard of our Lambretta scooter, but I was being dragged along. My brother-in-law saw this and wanted to call out so that my husband would stop the vehicle. I cautioned him against doing so since a sudden application of the brakes would have caused him to lose his balance; I was scared that he might fall off the scooter. My brother-in-law overtook my husband and asked him to slow down and stop. It was only then that my husband realized that I had fallen off and was being dragged. I must have fallen like a paratrooper. I sustained aberrations all over the left side of the body except my face. There was no major injury. When we returned home amidst all this drama, another drama was waiting to unfold.

Babuji was angry that we had got home late, but was equally shocked at my state. Just then, who should come but my commanding officer. After the usual pleasantries, he dropped a bombshell - that I had to proceed to Bangalore the next day to attend a course. I was not detailed for this course as I was the junior-most amongst all the officers. The officer who was officially detailed had managed to wriggle out, and I was made to fill in.

My husband tried his level best and thanks to his perseverance, he managed to reserve a berth for me from Delhi to Madras. Those days you had to go to Bangalore via Madras. There was no direct train from Delhi to Bangalore. The journey to Delhi from Ludhiana was unreserved. Imagine me, looking like a modern-day Rani Laxmi Bai! The left side of my body was swathed in bandages; I was carrying a few-months-old child in one hand and a steel trunk in the other. There was no seat available, so I had to stand for the duration of the journey. One of my fellow passenger's steel trunk, which was placed in the luggage compartment, slipped from the top and fell on me. I somehow reached New Delhi and boarded the train to Madras. I had a reserved berth thanks to my husband. Now the Goddess of Good Luck smiled on me. In the four-seater coach, three of my co-passengers were nursing officers from the army. They too were travelling to Bangalore. They took pity on me, seeing my condition, and looked after my son and me. My son was duly handed over to my brother-in-law, who was then employed in Gwalior. The nursing officers cleaned my wounds, dressed them and gave me antibiotic injections. They really took good care of me. Before we reached Bangalore, I was fighting fit thanks to their help.

Our vegetable garden

We had a sprawling vegetable garden in our backyard. *Babuji* was good at gardening and had basic knowledge of vegetable farming. Our Air Force station had organised classes for vegetable farming by the Punjab Agricultural University (PAU). The fertile land of Punjab and the farming classes were contributory factors for our vegetable and flower garden being adjudged 'the best' in the station.

Babuji followed a routine. Every morning, at 4 am, he would set out into the garden with his battalion, i.e. the gardener, my husband, *Ma* and I, and later, our new-born son was also included. *Babuji*, along with my husband and gardener, would dig the land. My mother-in-law and I used to weed and water the plots. We had bumper crops of potato, onion, garlic, *jeera, saunf* and many more. For the first time, I learnt how to preserve onions and garlic.

Irrespective of what time we got back from the hospital or a party, *Babuji* would knock on the door to wake us up. We had no choice but to get up; he would not tolerate any excuses. We just had to get up and start working in the garden. This was not to my liking, but I had no choice. When our elder son was born, he would lie in his *jhoola* (baby swing) and keep us company in the garden, looking at the birds chirping nearby and the butterflies darting by. *Babuji* used to sing nursery rhymes to him as he gardened. The baby enjoyed all these activities and used to laugh. To boost our gardening, we also had a small poultry farm to cater to our daily needs. Everything was fine except for getting up early in the morning after a late night. But we got used to; it was more than a military discipline! With our combined efforts, our garden bloomed and was judged the best.

Babuji and his elder grandson

Our elder son was born in New Delhi. After his naming ceremony on the tenth day, I was back home. Maybe I should attribute his sound habit of 'early to rise' to *Babuji's* training during his childhood in the vegetable garden. My elder son, his first grandson, was his pet - *aankhon ka taara*.

Culinary talent

Babuji was an excellent cook. He particularly excelled in preparing non-vegetarian dishes. You will be surprised to know that this Tambrahm, who had not touched onion and garlic, was regularly cooking meat, chicken and fish daily within three months of marriage. However, I was still a vegetarian, and I continue to be one till date. *Babuji* was fond of some special items which took a lot of time to prepare; to be honest, I did not find any of those dishes particularly tasty. One of them was *kosa chorchidi*, a dish that was essentially cooked with vegetable peels. It was not bad, but it was nothing exotic either. Whenever we had guests for dinner, *Babuji* would insist on preparing this dish. Our guests were mostly from Punjab and had never even dreamt of a dish made from vegetable peels. The guests used to wonder what the dish was initially and then laugh it off. But we became jokers in their eyes. Any amount of pleading with *Babuji* was to no avail. Finally, I let it pass.

The fridge

Our refrigerator was only a status symbol. *Babuji*, with his knowledge of physics, never let us keep anything in the fridge except for water and milk. He was right, as there was no electricity for most of the day. He believed in eating freshly cooked food. When you have a fridge, it is but natural to store the leftover food and consume it during the next meal. That never happened in our house. Each food item was freshly prepared. Our colleagues were surprised when they opened the fridge to find only milk and water. Summer in Punjab is extremely hot. The filled water bottles used to vanish in a jiffy. No one refilled the bottles except for *Babuji*. He used to crib a lot about this.

Music classes

The first song my father-in-law heard me sing was *chinechi tomar ye mon* (I have understood your heart) It is an *adhunik*

Bengali film song. I did not know the meaning of the song then. Later, when I learnt and understood Bengali, I felt embarrassed when I realized what exactly I had sung for my father-in-law! *Babuji* started teaching me music after we got married. He taught me Rabindra *sangeet*, Shyama *sangeet* and

Batiali songs. Today, the Bengalis believe me to be one of them thanks to my fluency in the language and my ability to sing Bengali songs.

There was no time for music classes, however. After dinner, we both would sit with a harmonium and he taught me songs for one or two hours. I was happy learning new things, and learning Bengali songs helped me to take part in the Durga *Puja* activities too. My value quotient increased manifold amongst Bengalis. Our music class was the talk of the town for many years. Even my youngest brother was taught a Bengali poem for recitation during Durga *Puja*. He went up on stage, recited the first line and forgot the rest. He started crying loudly. It was a miserable occasion for him and he remembers it till date.

Babuji, the disciplinarian

The minute I entered the house back from the hospital, I had to bathe and change before entering the kitchen or picking up my son. Good hygiene practice, please. After this, *Babuji* would leave my son in my care. I used to wonder why he was so heartless, not allowing me any rest. Now I understand. If the mother does not spend time with the child, how does the bond between mother and child develop? Spending quality time with the child is essential. When I was doing a course at AFMC almost every alternate day, I used to receive inland letters filled up and written on all the flaps in multi-colour. These were *Babuji's* instructions to me to do well in the course and to take care of my health. My colleagues used to tease me, thinking the letters were from my husband; they were quite shocked when they learnt that they were from my father-in-law.

Love for cinema

Babuji had to watch an English film once a week at our local cinema hall. On that day, he would wrap up all his activities quite early, dress up in white (as was customary) and cycle to the movie hall. We both requested him to take *Ma* with him to see the film, but he would never agree. He reasoned with us that she did not know English. It was male chauvinism at its peak.

The 1971 operations

One evening, as we were having dinner, the conversation veered to the then East Pakistan and how the Bengalis were suffering at the hands of West Pakistan. Somehow, I was dragged into the debate. I did not sympathize much with the east Pakistanis even though they were Bengalis; I felt sorry for the Indian soldiers. *Babuji* got annoyed and started shouting at me, saying that I did not understand Bengali culture. At this, I lost my cool and started arguing that Tamil was the oldest living language and culture in India. He was furious at my argument and decided to leave home in the dead of night. I realized my mistake and apologized profusely and managed to convince him to return to home.

Imminent war preparations

Soon after this, the station was declared a non-family station and the families were shifted to either their hometown or sent to their relatives or to a nearby safe civil area. As a result, *Babuji, Ma* and our son, who was about six months old then, were sent to Gwalior. My husband and I were looking after our respective wings and there was no one at home. Everything was kept ready for operations. I was the only lady at the station and I was with the medical wing along with my colleagues, looking after the war casualties. I was the privileged one who was permitted to go home once a week for my hair bath. I had beautiful hair at that time!

Babuji's last days

Suddenly, *Babuji* took ill during the middle of ops in Gwalior. We could not go immediately. He was admitted to the best hospital in Gwalior. Once the operations got over, we proceeded to Gwalior post haste. *Babuji* had slipped into coma by the time we reached. However, he recovered from his coma on December 26, recognised us all, and even gave us a firing as his pet grandson was not well dressed; he ordered us to buy a good dress for him. He also blessed us both saying that both of us would get the President's medal, a prediction that came true. The next day, he gathered us all together and was pleased to see his grandson smartly turned out. He sang *bhajans* (songs in praise of God) and asked us to join in. He passed away peacefully while listening to the *bhajans*. We felt miserable and all of us cried inconsolably. *Babuji* governed our family with an iron fist but gently.

Thus, the saga of a noble soul, *Babuji,* ended.

I wonder why the term 'in law' is used. I should be able to call my father-in-law the same as I call my father since he is like my father. Before marriage, the father and mother do so much to help their daughter stand on her own legs, and after marriage, it is the father-in-law and mother-in-law who guide her to be a part of the new family. My personal view is that the father-in-law should be called the same title as 'papa' (father), with the addition of elder or younger, as per the age of the relative. Being able to call one's in-laws 'papa' and 'mamma' will bring the young bride closer to her new family. This is my view and one may agree or disagree. In the present scenario, the situation may be different. I called my in-laws what my husband called them, and I was as close to them as their own sons and daughter.

The Love of My Life

"Janma, mrityu, bibaha, bidhatar hathe." This means 'your birth, marriage and death are in the hands of the Almighty'.

After a month at the Air Force Hospital in Secunderabad, we received 'breaking news' that Air Force was taking over MH Bangalore, and Air Force Hospital, Secunderabad was to be handed over to the Army. I was very happy, relieved and was looking forward to moving to Bangalore. In my wildest of dreams, I never imagined that I would be meeting my heart throb, my life partner, my best friend, philosopher and guide, my inspiration, all rolled into one: i.e., my future husband, on my very first day in Bangalore.

The First Encounter

On that momentous first day, my senior, Wing Commander Madam and I were walking along the officer's ward. We came across a very young and handsome patient, who had sustained a compound fracture of the right leg bones, (Tibia and Fibula). He was dressed in a pure white *kurta* and *pajama*; he held a guitar and was singing. Madam cautioned me, saying, "Don't speak to this officer. You keep away from him." At that time, I did not understand the reasons behind the statement. Maybe, thanks to her age and experience, she saw sparks flying between us which I did not sense. I used to wonder why she was being such a *khadoos* (bad-tempered person) by cautioning me not to talk to him.

Every day, he used to be propped up in a sitting posture outside the veranda and wish all the doctors passing by, including me; he would wish us 'Good Morning' with a pleasant smile. He was a very popular officer and had many well-wishers and girlfriends visiting him every day. He was made to sit up with his fractured leg in plaster, stretched out, singing Tagore's songs. His favourite song was *"Ei korecho bhalo nithur he..."*, meaning, "what you have done to me, my cruel Lord, it is for my good". In a hospital to be dressed up immaculately at 07.30 in the morning is near impossible, especially for a junior officer. You need all the help from everyone, right from the nursing officers, ward boys and *safaiwalas*. Remember, he was immobile with a plaster cast covering his entire right leg from hip to toes.

Falling in love

Because my senior had told me not to meet him, I made it a point to meet him as often as possible on some pretext or the other, amidst my busy internship duties. I had fallen in love with him at first sight without my knowledge. I was impressed by his looks, courage and his sense of duty towards his family. We had a lot of similarities and plenty of cultural differences. We both wanted to provide a comfortable life to our parents and look after them well in their old age. Also, we wanted to help in educating our brothers so that they would do better. In the short span of one month, after leaving Lucknow, I had met many young officers in Secunderabad, who had bragged about themselves and believed that they were exceptional. He was the first young officer I had met who wanted to help his family. I was impressed too that he had his feet firmly planted on mother earth. He was a topper from Banaras Hindu University and I had topped from Pune University. We were on similar wavelengths. Of course, we had a lot of differences too, which surfaced much later.

Till that point in my career, my only aim in life was to study hard and become a good doctor. I always wanted to become a cardiologist like Dr Padmavati, my role model. Maybe my hormones were raging. Also, this was the first time I was truly alone, and I was missing my parents, my good friends and my college, AFMC, Pune. I had no friends in Bangalore, no one to share my ups and downs. I was economically independent and belonged to the noble profession of Medicine. Possibly all these factors worked together to propel me into a different way of life.

I had time to look at young men and they too started looking at me. Suddenly, I felt I was swimming alone in the ocean against the current. I was not used to this situation.

Here was a very handsome man who spoke the very same language as me; he was someone I could understand; he was compassionate towards his people, wanting to do so much for his parents, brothers and sister. Our frequencies matched, and I think, within a few days, we decided that we would get married with our elders' blessings. Even though I knew very little about him at that point of time, I dared to accept that he was my man and took the bold decision. After we got married and lived together, many good and bad qualities in both of us surfaced. We faced our differences confidently and were very happy in our married life.

How did he land up in the hospital? He was then posted as Camp Commandant, Headquarters Training Command, Bangalore. He was rushing to the office at great speed on his Lambretta scooter (his one proud possession). He had an accident and was thrown off the scooter and his right leg hit the sharp edge of a culvert. He sustained a bad fracture of both the bones of the right leg. The accident took place on March 28, 1968 and I met him on April 01, 1968 for the first time. After three unsuccessful operations in Bangalore, the surgeons were contemplating amputating his right leg (below the knee). God Almighty helped him in the form of the then Air Officer Commanding in Chief (AOC-in-C) of Training Command. The AOC-in-C was very fond of him. He convinced the doctors at Air Force Hospital, Bangalore to shift him to the Military Hospital in Kirkee (the armed forces' biggest orthopaedic centre) for further treatment. He arranged for his airlift to the Military Hospital at Kirkee on or about April 10, 1968. He was under the care of a well-reputed orthopaedic surgeon.

We never went out together. We would only meet in the corridors of the officer's ward since he was immobile. We shared no coffees together, no picnics or dinners. But, we had both decided to tie the knot within those first ten days. I realized and understood that those in love need not meet one another, as they live in each other's hearts from the very beginning. In those ten days, I must have spoken to him for a total of 30 minutes. That is destiny. There was I, a pure, staunch Tamil Brahmin deciding to get married to a Bengali gentleman. When we got married in February 1969 in Bangalore, it was 'breaking news' at AFMC. Nobody believed it!

My husband was treated at the best centre of the armed forces. In those days, the essence of treatment was to align the fractured bones, immobilise them with a plaster cast and hang the leg over a pulley so that they reached the near-normal configuration over a period. As the leg is weight bearing, it is essential that the alignment must be near normal.

After he was airlifted to MH Kirkee, I was alone. I did not know whom to turn to for help, clarification or reassurance. It was the most miserable period of my life till then. As a child and young girl, my parents had always been there to guide and help me. When I joined college, there was Lizzie, my friend in need. During my medical college days, we were seven of us who shared every secret under the sun and we were always there for one another. Now, there was no one. I was the only unmarried lady doctor. The senior ladies were not interested in my problems and were very busy with their own issues. I was scared to talk to any young man. This was a period of huge emotional turmoil for me.

During the time when he was away at Pune, my parents wanted me to meet some armed forces doctors (prospective grooms) who were either in Bangalore or passing through Bangalore. The horoscopes were matched before they came to Bangalore. I had already decided on 'who' I wanted to marry. I was mortally scared of conveying that decision to my parents. Whenever the so-called prospective bridegrooms visited me, I immersed myself in attending to emergencies at the hospital. After three or four such instances, my parents realized that something was cooking in Bangalore.

Courtship

After about six months, the bones did unite with minimal angulation and some shortening.My, to-be husband came back to Bangalore in crutches in September 1968. I started meeting him *chupke chupke* (on the quiet) and going out. For two people in love, the world does not exist; only the two of them exist. There is no other thought in their minds. Not even how to manage life after the courtship. All those thoughts are swept away. That specific moment is most precious, most beautiful and you don't need to talk. The gaze and expressions convey all your feelings. He used to visit me in the hospital, and we would go out sometimes. He drove me to Nandi Hills on his famous Lambretta with the plaster in one leg and a crutch in the other! God knows how he balanced my weight too. We enjoyed that trip, and it is still fresh in my memory. When I see young couples, I remember those good old days.

The parents arrive

My parents arrived in Bangalore sometime in October-November 1968 to live with me till my internship was completed and was posted out of Bangalore. We hunted for a house. My colleague, who was already married, had rented a house very near the hospital. He was kind enough to let my parents live there. Provisioning started with our *madrasi* filter coffee powder, instead of the Nescafe of today. Luckily, Bangalore catered to *amma's* wishes and she was happy. After they settled down, I was scared to tell them about my wedding plans. However, my future husband was bold enough to take the initiative and conveyed our decision to get married. My parents were dead against us getting married in the beginning. Naturally so. It was unheard of in our community.

Now it was time to meet his parents. The first meeting was fraught with tension and was almost like a comedy of errors. As there was no news from his parents' side, despite several letters, my husband decided to go to Meerut himself and bring them over to Bangalore. He boarded the service aircraft and the aircraft started taxiing. At that point of time, I received a letter informing of their arrival. I immediately called him up and conveyed the message. As per custom, once the aircraft taxies, it does not stop or turn back. My husband requested the crew and they took pity on him and the aircraft returned to base.

We both rushed to the railway station to receive his parents on their arrival. My husband had briefed me, about how to recognise his parents. I quote, "My mother is a very thin, fair, beautiful lady draped in a traditional Bengali saree. With her will be my father. Always instructing and bullying my mother. He is of medium height, wheatish in complexion and has long hairs on his ears. So, you can recognise this couple easily". Both of us moved in opposite directions to spot them in the busy crowded platform.

Thanks to his description, I spotted them and we both brought them home. *Babuji* was very fond of music. My future husband had given me a cassette to learn some songs. From the collection, I had learnt a few songs though I did not know the meaning of even one song. As I have recounted earlier, the singing episode ended up in embarrassment, but *babuji* nevertheless congratulated me on learning the song, after a few awkward seconds. At that time, I did not realize that big challenges awaited me in the future.

Dissimilarities and disagreements

The disagreements started on the very first day his parents arrived. Initially, over tea, we exchanged pleasantries. When dinner time arrived and *Babuji* ordered for fish, the situation exploded. My mother was a pure vegetarian and would not budge a micron. She insisted, "No fish at home." The same evening, we both ran around searching for a house for his parents and found one. I think people took pity on us and helped us in all possible ways.

Both the sides would not budge and there were lots of arguments and counter-arguments. Some ended amicably and some in severe bitterness. The very first incident was about eating fish and other non-vegetarian food. This was the main reason for both the parties to be accommodated separately. The second was my being in the Air Force and my job as a doctor. *Babuji*, was not very happy with a professional *bahu* and that too someone working in the Air Force. Another factor, which was very important to them, was my complexion. I was not fair by any standard; rather, I was on the darker side and my husband was very fair and handsome. I do not remember how long these conflicts continued. But, over time, both sides realized that the two of us were committed to one another and there was no escape for them except to get us married.

Fortunately for us, they thrashed out all the issues. And our wedding was fixed for February 13, 1969. Many of our friends were skeptical as we belonged to different cultural backgrounds and the wedding date was 13, which is not considered an auspicious number. Everyone predicted that the marriage would not last for more than a year. But, we proved all the predictions wrong. We were happily married for more than 45 years and I still feel he is always with me even after he left for his heavenly abode.

The Wedding

We had wedding ceremonies in both south Indian style and Bengali style. *Babuji* had commanded me not to leave the house for one week before the wedding as it was their custom. What could I do? During internship, you are not allowed any leave. Still, they had granted me two days casual leave for the wedding. This meant that I had to go to hospital until the day I got married, something which *babuji* did not like. But, he had no choice. Apart from that, I had to go with my parents to invite all my friends from the hospital as they did not know anyone. This too was frowned upon by *babuji*. This time, I had no choice. On the evening of the engagement (day prior to wedding), I, along with my parents, had landed up at our Commanding Officer's house. At the same time my fiancé, along with *babuji and ma*, also landed up at the same place. And, *babuji* was really upset. Again, there was no choice. Finally, on Thursday morning, our marriage was solemnised in the south Indian style with me draped in a traditional nine-yard saree.

The same evening, after the reception, the Bengali wedding ceremony took place with both of us wearing *topur* (the headgear made of pith which is white). I was dressed in a beautiful Banarasi saree which I still treasure.

As my husband and I were the only people who knew something about Bangalore, we had to run around to organise the wedding feast. There were no catering services those days. You had to procure the provisions, and the cooks would prepare the items as required. How were we to get the rations? Both our parents had no time and did not know anything about the city. We both ran around on our prized possession, the Lambretta, and bought all the ration items. Of course, our friends also pitched in. So, the morning breakfast and lunch were served in traditional style on banana leaves. After the reception at the Officer's mess, the dinner was served in stylish crockery with non-vegetarian dishes. Later, the traditional Bengali ceremony took place. Thus, after nearly three months of arguments, counter-arguments and cultural clashes, it all ended on a happy note.

After the wedding, my father gave me one simple piece of advice: "Never complain about 'your' family and try and do your best for your family. Never come back crying to us." Our horoscopes were never matched.

The IAF was destiny for us

While at Secunderabad, I had applied for a para jumping course in Agra. My application from the hospital had reached Training Command. My future husband had not forwarded the application because he felt compassion towards Flying Officer S Padmavathy, whom he had never seen or heard of. He did not want her fracturing her bones. He did not know me then and I had no idea as to who Flying Officer SN Bandopadhyay was. After marriage, he admitted that he was responsible for my name not being included in the para jumping course and asked me to reapply for it. However, I declined the offer as I was already married, and family was my priority.

Nevertheless, I had always wanted to fly free in the open blue sky above. That was the main reason why I joined the Air Force. The Air Force brought us together. If it were not for the Indian Air Force (IAF), maybe we would have never met one another. Thus, I feel, I was destined to be an Air Force officer, the lady in 'blue'. Throughout our married life and even after retirement, this bond of the blue uniform was very strong for both of us. We both felt indebted to the Air Force and had a wonderful life serving the IAF. It is the IAF which gave both of us VSMs together at the same Investiture Parade in 1973 - a first in the world. The IAF is responsible for my reputation and fame in being the FIRST LADY AIR MARSHAL in the world. The IAF gave us a happy married life. Even on the day of my husband's funeral, the Air Force gave him a hero's send-off in true IAF style.

Jai Hind.

Asha - a Ray of Hope

I was named Padmavathy by my parents and my official name in the school records was S Padmavathy. What is this 'S' doing there? Where and what is my surname? Am I ashamed of my surname? These were some of the thoughts that cropped up in other people's minds when they came to know me, especially in north India. The 'S' in my name stands for my father's name, V Swaminathan, where 'V' is his father's name. The next thing people want to know is my surname. I think people from the south, especially from Tamil Nadu, were quick enough to realize that it was better to drop the caste name or surname. We do not usually use any surname. My surname is Iyer, but I did not know this when I was a child. My name is in the news nowadays because of a movie titled 'Padmavathy' starring Deepika Padukone in the lead role. Dr Soumya Swaminathan is the first Indian to be appointed to the second highest position at the World Health Organisation. My name is popular in the entertainment as well as in the medical field.

The concept of surnames

At school, I did not face any issues as it was a south Indian school where no one used surnames. The few north Indian students admitted to our school were the ones who made us aware of the concept of surnames. They had a tough time answering our questions regarding their fathers' names, village names, house names and many other such names. In effect, a south Indian name, if written fully, represents the entire postal address of the individual. Let's take the example of the famous Bharat Ratna MS Subbalakshmi, 'M' stands for her village name; 'S' stands for her husband's name-Mr. Sadashivan, and her own name is Subbalakshmi, the name of Goddess Lakshmi. Is it not beautiful?

Our youngest niece was admitted to a school at Chennai. Her name was Surabhi Banerjee. Her friends volleyed her with questions. What is your father's name? Why don't you write your father's name? Who is Banerjee? Which Banerjee are you related to? The poor child had no answers to these questions as she did not understand them at all. During my early college days, these questions had frequently cropped up and many of my collegemates made fun of me. I did not know the answers initially but discovered them later and carried on. In my view, the best system of naming is what is prevalent in Western India. They have the first name (one's name), the middle name (father's/husband's name) and the last name, which is the caste name.

India's unity in diversity is something you get a feel of at every step of your life. In this process, you learn a lot about the cultural history of India. But, of course, thanks to this very diversity, there are times when the bullying can be intolerable. You must stand up and face the bullies when they repeatedly make fun of you about your name. You should learn adequate life skills to overcome these minor irritants. I did that and succeeded in swatting away minor irritants like bullying over my name.

I faced the first and last interview of my life during my admission process for entering the sacred portal of my medical college, the Armed Forces Medical College (AFMC). They asked me, what to me was, a very tough question. What is your name? My answer: I sobbed. Why? I was petrified when I saw so many uniformed service officers. My tongue went dry, my brain stopped thinking. The stress of seeing so many uniformed officers at the same time was too much for me to bear and I burst out crying. When the rarest "second chance" was given to me, I proved my worth and was selected for the college.

Mispronouncing my name

Even after this blooper, I made it to Armed Forces Medical College. Here, the ordeal unfolded in a very funny way. Most of my teachers at the medical college were Bengalis, from the eastern part of India. They had a funny way of pronouncing my beautiful name. They called out my name during roll call as 'Poddabothy'. I used to be seated in the front row, but I never answered the roll call as I did not hear my name being called out. The professor used to ask me, why I did not respond to his roll call? I could never fathom that my name had been murdered like that! I repeatedly impressed upon them that my name was Padmavathy and would spell out my name. They would say "yes, yes", but the next day they would mispronounce my name all over again. Finally, I got used to it and began responding to the roll call even though I hated my name being mispronounced. What I did not know at that point of time was that I was going to marry a Bengali later in my life. It was only after marriage that I understood why my name became *Poddabothy* in Bengali.

After I graduated from medical college, I completed my internship at Air Force Hospital, Bangalore. Soon after, I married Flying Officer Sati Nath Bandopadhyay, my heartthrob who, as I mentioned earlier, was a Bengali. I am not sure, but maybe I was one of the few who married soon after the internship. Since we had mutually decided to get married, it raised many eyebrows. In those days, almost all marriages were arranged by the elders. All my classmates were surprised and shocked to hear the news as I was a staunch *madrasi*. No one, including myself, believed that I would marry a Bengali. I think, I started believing in God from that day.

Now I can tell you why my teachers called me 'Podda'. In Bengali, if there is a compound word like 'dma', the second syllable is not pronounced, and the first syllable is doubled. In Bengali, 'va' is pronounced as 'ba'. That is how my name changed to 'Poddabothy' while on roll call by my Bengali teachers at AFMC.

Changing my name

When I got married, I knew I would have to change my name to Mrs. Bandopadhyay, which was customary. This change in name involved a lot of paperwork as I was an Armed Forces Officer. A gazette publication was required. I knew all the requirements and worked on it earnestly. I did not look like a Bengali, even if you stretched your imagination to the sky. I was keen that at least my name should indicate that I am the wife of SN Bandopadhyay.

Interestingly, in my husband's family, the rest of the menfolk were Banerjee, except for my husband. The reason is that he started his schooling in West Bengal. The school leaving certificate would always print as Bandopadhyay even though the admission form was filled up as Banerjee. The only choice one had was to choose the spelling from amongst various choices: Bandyopadhyay, Bandopadhyaya, Bandopadhyay and many more versions. His father chose Bandopadhyay, so I chose it too. It was quite funny because my youngest brother, who was then eight years old, could not pronounce this tongue twister of a name.

Finally, my name was officially changed to Padma Bandopadhyay. I did feel bad to lose the 'vathy' portion of my name. But I had no choice because in the Air Force, a nameplate with such a long name is not accepted. The nameplate said P Bandopadhyay. My original name was contracted to a single syllable, 'P'.

An unofficial name

Soon after marriage, in some families, it is customary to change the daughter-in-law's name. I was christened with another name although it was not official. My in-laws christened me 'Asha'. I wondered then as to why they had chosen the name 'Asha' for me. Anyway, I was quite happy with the name as I imagined myself as the famous singer, 'Asha Bhonsle'. So, what if I was no more 'S Padmavathy'. To allay my curiosity, I did ask my husband why this name was chosen. He had no answers. So, I gathered courage and asked *babuji* why he had changed my name to Asha. Here is the poignant story of my name change. *Babuji* had four sons and one daughter. As was the custom, the elder son was educated in an engineering college. By the time the eldest son graduated, b*abuji* had retired from service. My elder brother-in-law was the first to choose a bride outside the community, hence starting the tradition of "love marriages" in our family. He fell in love with a beautiful Punjabi girl and they got married. *Babuji* was against the marriage initially but later agreed for his son's happiness. Soon after, the couple left for UK where they both did very well. When my elder brother-in-law was at the pinnacle of his professional achievement, cruel fate snatched him away from all of us. Fortunately, *babuji* passed away before his sad end.

When his son left for the UK, *Babuji* missed him terribly but kept the sadness to himself. My husband is the second son. When he expressed his desire to marry me, *Babuji* was crestfallen. Not only was I not a Bengali, but I was also an Armed Forces doctor. To him, that was a deadly combination. After discussions and plenty of emotional drama, he agreed for our wedding. The saving grace was that we both belonged to the same caste. But, he was praying day and night that I should be a good *bahuma*. He fondly named me 'Asha', hoping and praying that all his dreams would be fulfilled through me. I do not know how successful I was in fulfilling all his dreams, but he was happy during the time he was alive, which was for about two years after our marriage. He was at his happiest with his eldest grandson. The child too was very fond of him. He is no more there to call me 'Asha' but all the relatives still call me by that name and I am very proud of it. I could at least fulfil some of his dreams and give a few moments of happiness to my *babuji*.

What's in a name?

Our elder son was named Sainath by my mother as she was a devotee of *Sri Saibaba*. *Ma* named him 'Gopal Krishna' as he was dark complexioned like me. And, *Babuji* named him 'Amiya', meaning nectar. This is his official name. In our exuberance, we both spelt his name as Omeo to rhyme with Romeo. Amiya is pronounced as Omeo because in Bengali, 'A' is pronounced as 'O'. When he topped all the medical entrance tests, many young boys and girls congratulated him. As the spelling ended with 'a', some had mistaken him for a girl. In South India, a boy's name ends with 'n', 'm', etc. and not with 'a'.

Every language has its own twists and turns which makes it unique. A lot of love, hope, prayers and many more dreams of parents are woven around a name. In the olden days, we used to be named after Gods and Goddesses. This was because it was believed that even if you call the Lord once, just before you reach his lotus feet, 'He' will bless you. We human beings are always attached to family, wealth, power and many more things. By default, if you call your child's name on your deathbed, God will take care of you and bless you. Of course, everything depends upon your belief or faith. There is no scientific proof backing any of this.

What's in a name? Everything, I feel.

Amiya - the Nectar

Amiya's birth

I was very keen to be a mother, a cherished dream for most women. However, my husband was not too keen as we had a lot of family commitments to settle before we could take up the responsibility of bringing up a child. I told my husband that *Babuji* and *Ma,* who were living with us then, would be very happy to have a grandchild. They would enjoy spending happy times with the grandchild. I also told him that they would be of great help in bringing up the child. After many 'ifs' and 'buts', I was going to be a mother. As there was no obstetrician nearby, I had to travel 30 km to reach the nearest obstetrician. To ensure that I wouldn't miss my appointments, I would rush there in a jeep in my uniform. By the time I reached the hospital, my hair would be all dishevelled, and my uniform would be a crumpled mess. So, my first fantasy of decking up like the other ladies for antenatal check-ups was completely dashed!

The obstetrician was a German lady and her dedication to duty was matchless. She was an excellent doctor. As a uniformed person, I was very proud of my discipline and dedication to duty. But I was no match to her. She was very kind, and would reassure me whenever I had any doubts. Even if I arrived late due to the pressures of my work, she would wait for me despite her extremely busy schedule. The obstetrician was my friend, philosopher and guide at this stage, to whom I unburdened all my worries as there was no one else I could talk to about my problems or misgivings.

Explaining pregnancy to others as a doctor is very different from being an expectant mother yourself. All your textbook and hearsay knowledge are of no use. You must feel it, experience it and go through the highs and lows of pregnancy. There was no one at home to talk to. I was not comfortable talking to my mother-in-law about pregnancy-related issues. My husband was too busy with his work and unit duties. I too did not have much time to deliberate about the subject as I was very busy with my household chores and official duties. In those days, I used to do the cooking at home in addition to performing my hospital duties. The reason I had to do the cooking was owing to the non-availability of a Bengali cook. *Babuji* was very strict in all these matters. At hospital too, I was extremely busy as I had started the family wing. I was taking care of most of the uncomplicated deliveries. This meant long working hours, and many a time, I was kicked by patients in my abdomen. This was not willful. When the ladies were undergoing labour and were in pain, they were not aware of what was happening. Thankfully, all this physical activity helped me later during my delivery.

The child's complexion

I had a neighbour who was also my assistant. She used to advise me not to drink too much coffee or tea. She would tell me to drink a lot of orange juice instead, so that the child would be fair. Well, neither did I heed her advice, nor did I believe in all these vague instructions. Our elder son is very much like me in terms of both complexion and looks. Maybe, I should have listened to her advice!

Maternity leave

In those days, lady medical officers were not authorised maternity leave. They had to adjust the child's delivery within their annual leave. In the case of nursing officer, they had to quit uniformed service once they got married. In addition to all this, that year, everyone's leave was cancelled because of the impending war. How could I plan my delivery? There was no other way out of this problematic situation except for my *amma* to come and help us. My in-laws requested my mother to come over to look after me and she did. However, the obstetrician attending to me had to leave for Germany due to a sudden commitment. I requested for leave and was granted 10 days casual leave as a special case. Promptly, my husband packed my mother and me off to Delhi. As soon as I arrived in Delhi, I went for a check-up - my first and last one in Delhi. My Professor at AFMC was the obstetrician at Delhi and he confirmed that everything was fine.

A quick delivery

The day after my arrival in Delhi, I was grinding for *idli* batter for the next day's breakfast on the grinding stone. There's a reason why I am emphasising these minor facts: to underscore the importance of physical exercise. The more physically active you are, the easier it is to bear the labour pains. Not only that, you will also be healthier in the long run. That Sunday afternoon, I began to feel slight pain. "*Rahu Kalam*" (the inauspicious period of the day) was from 4:30 pm to 6:00 pm. Do remember that *amma* was a firm believer of this. She started praying and as soon as the *Rahu Kalam* was over, she hired a taxi and we left for Military Hospital (the present-day Army Hospital R&R) at Delhi cantonment from Gole market. At about 8 pm, I suddenly developed strong pains and, without much warning, by 8:30 pm, I delivered a normal healthy boy. The duty nursing officer was just wheeling me into the labour room but before I reached there, I delivered our son. Everyone was astonished.

The labour was short simply because I was healthy and physically very active till the date of delivery. My advice to all pregnant ladies is to please continue your routine physical activity including normal exercises and specific yoga *asanas*. Please consult your doctor always. Do not eat for TWO and do not while away your time. If you follow this simple advice, you will have a normal and easy delivery. Recently, a survey was conducted which revealed that too many 'C' sections were being carried out although for many patients, there were no clinical indications. I firmly believe that one must always encourage normal delivery under a doctor's care.

Our son was almost bald when he was born. *Amma* would give him an oil massage and then bathe him in hot water. The little fellow enjoyed it immensely and would promptly fall asleep after the oil bath. On the tenth day of his birth, we had the *Namkaran* (naming ceremony) for him, after which we left for Punjab. My husband received us at the station and we drove back home in our newly-acquired second-hand Fiat car.

Driving the car

My husband bought the car so that I could come home from work and feed my son. Hence, he insisted that I learn to drive the car. He would ask me to come for driving lessons. I would always be ready with some silly excuses like stomach ache, pain in the legs and feet and many more. Just like a kid attending nursery school for the first time! Finally, he gave up. I never learnt driving. Net result? I never came home to feed my son. The purpose of buying the car was totally defeated.

Bringing up the child

The credit for our son's upbringing goes totally to our *babuji*. We, the parents, made special appearances, that's all! When I entered the house with our son, he took the child in his lap and from that day on, he became *Babuji's* favourite. Our son was the centre of life in the household with all of us orbiting around him with the *suthradar* (remote controller) being *babuji*. The baby's bathing ritual changed. In Delhi, he used to have hot water baths, with hot water being poured especially over his bald head. My *Ma* insisted that he should have cold water poured on his head so that skull bones would get stronger. I do not know the rationale of either hot or cold water. But I let them do what they wanted. After all, my *Ma* had brought up her brothers and sisters and her own children. She had more experience than me. I had book knowledge, but *Ma* had hands-on experience. *Babuji*, the *sutradar,* was always there to do course correction.

Toilet training

Have you ever heard of a newborn not wetting the bed? The day I came home with our elder son, *babuji* started toilet training him. He would wake up every two hours - and wake all of us up if we were at home - and toilet train the baby. It is a record that he never wet the bed during his childhood. *Babuji* was very fond of him as he was the eldest grandchild in the family. Our son too was very fond of him. The minute he saw him or heard him, he would make happy faces, squeal and laugh and try to move. Later, he used to dance when he saw him. After the birth of our son, life was very peaceful and happy for all of us. But, no one facet of life continues for long and b*abuji* passed away soon after.

Breaking feeding bottles

Feeding our son was an ordeal. All the feeding bottles in those days were made of glass and were boat-shaped; he would kick them away and they would break. Finally, we decided to feed him through the age-old *junuk*, a feeding cup with a long narrow sprout. *Babuji* was an expert in feeding the child. He used to drape himself in an old tattered *lungi,* put the child on his lap and place his legs over the child so that he could not kick. During every feed, our son would cry, causing him to take deep breaths; when he did so, the milk was forced in. However, he was quite the little crook! Once the feeding was over and he had been burped, he was made to sit up; at this point, he used to vomit out all the milk. That was the reason for babuji's attire. The whole scene was no less fiery than a battlefield. Despite this daily battle to feed him his milk, he grew up to be quite healthy.

Our milkman, Major Singh, named him Gurdayal Singh as he used to sit outside and wish him *"Sat Sri Akal"*. The milkman would give us almost half a litre of extra milk for free for the child, saying, *"Munde de vaste."*

A naughty baby

Our son was introduced to solid food very soon when he was around six months old. We used to eat our meals at the dining table. This mischievous monkey would be sitting in the centre. Somehow or the other, he would lurch towards my youngest brother-in-law's plate and proceed to eat from it. He would eat half the food and throw the remaining half. My brother-in-law used to be furious. It was a sight to watch!

What's in a name

Our son's pet name was Gompa. At that time, we did not know what the word *'gompa'* meant. As he was a roly-poly and healthy, we called him gompa. Much later, I came to know that *'gompa'* referred to Buddhist *monasteries*. He was growing up well under the care of his grandparents. My husband and I were busy with our respective work and made special appearance sometimes to look after him.

Hygiene please

When I returned from office every day, *babuji* would insist on me having a bath before picking up the child. I used to be dead tired and starving. I used to secretly curse *babuji* for being so strict. Today, I realize how important that precautionary measure was, to prevent hospital infections. I am sorry to say that we Indians as a community do not care much about infections or hygiene.

While working at the hospital, it was common to see a crowd of people sitting on the patient's bed after the lady had delivered. The crowd used to be even larger if the newborn was a male child. The whole village would turn up to express their joy and give their blessings. The poor lady could not enjoy a minute of rest. She could not feed the baby in peace. When I used to shoo them out, they would get angry with me. Many a time they have fought with me. Some of the not-so-well-to-do of the village would come visiting wearing dirty clothes and take the child in their lap. It used to make me furious but not much can be changed by just shouting. People should become aware of hygiene and sanitation aspects, and their mindset must change.

Dressing up my son

Ma always dressed up Amiya in fancy frocks. He had by now grown beautiful curly hair and was a very cute baby. We ensured that he had all his vaccinations on time. We also maintained a diary about his day-to-day activities and milestones, such as when he first smiled, when he first recognised us, when he turned over for the first time, when he sat up, etc.

When a healthy baby show was held in Punjab, he was judged as the best child and was to receive a gift hamper. The presentation ceremony was in Chandigarh. *Ma* would not let us take the child there. She was scared that the evil eye would be cast on him. Finally, the gift hamper arrived by post. *Ma* was terrified of the evil eye. Even in the unit, when somebody asked her whether he was a boy or girl, she would unashamedly reply that he was her granddaughter. When confronted, she would tell us that girls could ward off the evil eye better than boys. I could never understand her logic and used to laugh it off.

In the garden

You could see the joy on his face the minute he spotted b*abuji*; he would even start dancing! Wasps feared Amiya as he used to hit them with his pudgy baby hands!

In the rain

My husband was very fond of rain. When it rained, we would pick up our son, put him in the car, load his commode on top of the car (as in Piku cinema) drive down to the nearby canal and stay put there. The raindrops falling on the roof of the car used to make rhythmic sounds that were very soothing. My husband would recite nursery rhymes in Bengali about the monsoon and the little fellow would be ecstatic. He would laugh wholeheartedly and squeal with happiness. We both enjoyed the rains with our son many times. Now, only memories of those wonderful times are left. My husband is no more. The little boy has grown up to be a practising psychiatrist. I am sure he does not remember how much happiness he gave us amidst our struggles in those days. Babies and children are a joy forever.

School experiences

Stay at Avadi

When we were posted to Avadi, Amiya was admitted to the local nursery school. He had a tricycle and would cycle to the school with his *tiffin* box and water bottle. He enjoyed the two hours at school, playing with other kids. I had to leave for a professional course to Lucknow for nearly three months. My husband and *Ma* were with him. During this period, this happy, healthy, cheerful child fell prey to pneumonia and was admitted to the nearby Military Hospital. The one and only treatment then was penicillin injections. My poor little son was given four injections a day and was practically alone at the hospital. His father was busy in the office; once he was home, he had to look after *Ma*. He could only spend a few hours with Amiya who was just two years old then. My senior officer helped us and spent time with our son till my husband could make it to the hospital. 'Thank you' was too small a word to express our heartfelt gratitude. My senior recited nursery rhymes in Bengali to divert his mind from the agonising pain of the penicillin injections.

Frank Anthony Public School, Bangalore

I was posted in Bangalore and was a student officer. Our elder son was admitted into the prestigious Frank Anthony Public School in Bangalore. His uniform had a Tie. I did not know how to knot a tie. My uniform then was saree and blouse without a 'tie'. My husband was away on a course. For the first few days, mother and son would rush to the neighbour's house requesting their help in knotting the tie. Later, I bought a tie with an elastic band, so that he could just slip it through.

He was not allotted the school bus. I used to drop him at school at 07.00 hours after a breakfast of bread and butter. All three meals comprised mostly bread, butter and eggs. Every night, the poor kid would ask me what I was cooking for the next day. My answer was the same. I felt sad and angry at myself; I also felt depressed. He carried two lunch boxes. One for his lunch break, another to eat after his junior school closed. He would sit with the *chowkidar* (security guard) till I picked him up at 5 pm after my classes were over at the institute. What a test of patience for a four-year-old! Till date, I admire my little boy who at the tender age of four would wait patiently for me for about four hours.

Amiya did not know a word of English then. He had a tough time in understanding English. English was the 'Lingua Franca' in the school. His lack of knowledge of English was another factor. He used to come back crying from school. It was very tough on him, but he picked up the language over a period of six months. Thankfully, children learn fast.

A role model

Our next stop was DSSC at Ooty where he was admitted to Brindavan Public School. From this point on, he started topping his class. We were then posted out to a forward airbase.

Our Gompa was always a responsible kid. I strongly feel it's because we both drilled into him that he was the eldest in the family and it was his duty to look after his brothers and sisters. We told him that he should set a shining example for them to follow. He is a glowing role model to not only the children but the entire family. Gompa was a topper in all activities and used to win the shield for the best student of the school year after year. What a great feeling it was and how proud we felt. Gompa always took care of his younger brother; he taught him whatever needed to be taught and would take him along when he went to play with his friends. Our younger son followed in Gompa's footsteps; he too was a darling of the school and was a topper as well. The station used to comment that the Banerjee clan was sweeping away all the medals.

Lunch at school

By now we had a full-time servant named Sharada, a spinster. When she went on leave during the winter months, my husband and I would share the housework. My favourite chore was taking lunch for the children to school. I used to carry the *tiffin* box packed with tasty, hot homemade food cooked by me along with a small *dhurrie* (carpet) for them to sit on. I would cycle to the school. When the school bell rang announcing the lunch break, the children would come running, gobble a mouthful of food, and then run and play. They used to finish the *tiffin* in a jiffy. I used to be so happy watching them eating heartily, playing and enjoying themselves. I think this was one of the few memories, I still recall and enjoy.

Kendriya Vidyalaya

Our next stop was Pune. The boys were admitted to the Kendriya Vidyalaya, Pune. Both the boys topped their respective classes. On Saturdays, I used to bring reference books from AFMC library home, and mark the relevant portions to be copied. I could not write fast as my thumb used to pain. Amiya used to copy the notes for me. Maybe this spark ignited the desire in him to become a doctor... I wonder. My sincere thanks to our son who helped me. He also continued to look after his younger brother.

Amiya becomes a doctor

Our next station was Bangalore, where they were admitted to Kendriya Vidyalaya, Hebbal, Bangalore. Amiya topped the school and topped all the medical entrance examinations, National Talent Search Examination (NTSE) and TOEFL. At this point, he was a hero! He chose to join All India Institute of Medical Sciences (AIIMS) at Delhi. After he graduated, he did his Post Graduate

Diploma in Psychiatry from the prestigious National Institute of Mental health and Neuro Sciences (NIMHANS), Bangalore and MD Psychiatry from AIIMS. Today, he is a leading psychiatrist, known for his humane and sympathetic approach towards his patients. He is happily married to his college colleague who is a gynaecologist and we have two loving grandsons.

Looking after me

As a senior citizen and a mother, I could not have asked the Almighty for anything better than our son Amiya and daughter in law Dr. Neelam Banerjee. They take care of me, look after my needs and all my hospital trips. As a child, he was a source of perennial joy and today, as an adult, he is a great source of support to me. God bless Amiya and Neelam.

The Adorable Lady Medical Officer *(LMO)*

The hospital where I was posted after my internship was the first in the chain of evacuation. The hospital had two General Duty Medical Officers (GDMO) (non-specialist); one was my Commanding Officer and the other was me. There were Aviation Medicine specialists to look after the pilots. I entered the portals of the hospital full of enthusiasm. I was excited to put into practice all that I had learnt during my college days and internship, of course with discretion. As far as gynaecology and obstetrics were concerned, I was quite confident of conducting normal deliveries and carrying out caesareans under the guidance of a gynaecologist.

The nearest service hospital was 90 km away. I felt sorry for the ladies travelling 90 km for routine *antenatal* (during pregnancy) check-ups in a *three-tonner* vehicle in the extreme summers and winters of North India. There was no seating arrangement for the ladies. Sometimes, bare benches were provided. I was really upset. I was of the firm belief that this pitiable state had to change. I continuously requested the Commanding Officer (CO) to let me establish a family ward where I could admit ladies for normal deliveries and children for minor ailments. His words still ring in my ears. He said, I quote, "You are not a specialist and you should not undertake all this. There may be legal complications." Since I was young and inexperienced in medical rules and regulations, I begged him to allow me to conduct normal deliveries and treat patients for common clinical conditions. My consistent persuasion finally paid off; he relented and allowed me to set up a makeshift family ward. And there I was, a young energetic doctor who was aiming to 'touch the sky with glory" winning her first hurdle.

Conventionally, a lady doctor, when posted...... looked after the family and children of all service personnel. The designation was Lady Medical Officer (LMO); it was not official though. All cases concerning women and children were referred to the LMO. Male doctors never treated them. It was not really the fault of the male doctors; the ladies were unwilling to be examined by a male doctor and insisted on lady doctors. The male doctors were fine with the situation and never tried to explain or convince the ladies that all doctors were the same, whether male or female. For me, it was a win-win situation. I used to work very hard, almost four times as hard as the other officers, but I enjoyed my work. My internship training helped me a lot.

After my constant persuasion, the obstetrician posted in a nearby civil hospital agreed to help me in carrying out caesarean operations at our hospital as and when required. Our hospital had the necessary equipment required for all major surgeries but no trained manpower. I could conduct the operations, but my boss insisted on getting a specialist doctor and correctly so. I used to perform the operations under her guidance. Thanks to this initiative, the poor lady patients did not have to travel 90 km to reach the military hospital. I felt it was God's gift to have the help of the local specialist. This arrangement worked for nearly two years till she resigned from her job and left for United Kingdom.

Hospital ambulance

In addition to the other problems we faced, the rickety ambulances of those days were notorious for frequent breakdowns. The ambulance was a converted one-tonner which often was under some repairs. Those days, we did not have coolants and good petrol. In summer, we had to stop intermittently and add ice cubes or cold water. Otherwise, the engine would get heated up and stop. In winter, we had to push, push and push to start the vehicle; sometimes we used to pour hot water to start the ambulance. The station used to comment that, "the ambulance kills more patients than the doctors". But my ambulance drivers were the best human beings, I've known. Both the ambulance drivers were ex-servicemen. They took great care of me when

I accompanied serious patients to the nearby military hospital either during daytimes or at night. Whenever the ambulance would stop, they would assure me that it would start soon; they would fetch hot tea for me even if we were in the middle of nowhere. I would be busy attending to emergencies during the journey. Despite all the hiccups, I was confident of travelling with them and no one else. Even if they were off duty, they used to come if I needed them to drive the ambulance as they were aware that I would not go with any other driver. What great human beings they were. I still remember them even though I have forgotten their names. Probably, one of them was Sardar Amar Singh,

The family ward

I performed surgeries for the family planning program. Our unit was adjudged 'the best' in Family Planning and we received a trophy. I used to slog from morning to evening; then there were night emergencies and other duties. I thoroughly enjoyed my work and received lot of respect and adulation from the people who respected me as a good doctor. What else can a doctor aspire for?

An ad-hoc family ward was set up in a covered corridor and the open sides were blocked with thick curtains. There was one rickety fan which produced more noise than circulating air. I could admit about ten to fifteen inpatients and I was thrilled beyond measure. The pilgrimage of ladies to the far-off hospital came to an end. Only complicated cases were referred there. I used to conduct *antenatal* clinics on Thursdays and the families of serving and ex-servicemen used to come from far and near, using all modes of transportation from walking to tractors during the extreme summers and winters. They never addressed me as 'doctor'. Instead, they used to call me *Bibiji* with great affection.

Legal problems

Things were going well, and I was enjoying my work. Suddenly, a legal problem cropped up for no fault of mine. One day, an air warrior (in those days known as Flight Sargent) reported at the hospital for his son's eye problem. I admitted the child as he was suffering from an eye infection. I admitted the mother too, as the child was very young. I put them in one corner of the makeshift ward to isolate the child and prevent the infection from spreading to other patients. The air warrior wanted to avail some leave as he could not manage his duties and look after the rest of the family. I spoke to his Commanding Officer, requesting him to grant him a few days leave so that he could look after his family in the absence of his wife. That too was granted. I have mentioned before that I used to conduct antenatal clinics on Thursdays. I can recall this incident clearly even after the passage of so many years. That specific Thursday, the then Air Chief Marshal, had inspected our station for operational preparedness and after his visit it was declared as *Admin day*, meaning it was a holiday for everyone, except for those on essential duties.

I continued with my work as several ladies, who were pregnant, had come from quite far. I felt it was my bounden duty to take care of them. The examination chamber was a small cubicle partitioned with curtains on all sides. It was a makeshift arrangement till the permanent building came up. The air warrior was hovering around outside the chamber as he wanted to speak to me. I kept requesting him very politely to wait outside till I completed my check-up of the lady in the room. I told him I would talk to him once I had finished. But he refused to heed my pleas; he barged in, and I asked him to get out. I was furious and upset. After completing the examination, I came out and found the administration's boss standing in one corner, discussing something with another officer. I approached him and reported what had happened. He said he would take care of it and that I should not worry. I continued examining the other women and left for home in the evening. At this point of time, the commanding officer of my hospital was away on leave and another officer had come in to *officiate* as the Commanding Officer. When I reached home dead tired, I received a phone call from the *guard room* that there was a ROG against me. I did not even know what ROG stood for. ROG is the short form of *Redress of Grievance*. The ROG was filed by the same Flt Sgt whom I had helped. He had written a whole lot of pointless complaints against me. I was shocked, to say the least. I had not even known about these things. Neither in medical college nor during my internship had these subjects been brought up. Now, I remembered the first words of my CO, who had advised me against starting a family wing. How prophetic those words were!

But, I have never been the type to give up. The enquiry went on for nearly a year. The charge against me was not medical negligence but wasting government money in looking after his wife in the hospital. I went through all the service enquiries at a very early stage of my service career. However, I never learnt my lessons, and many a time, I have landed in a soup.

Innovation and a heart-warming recovery

I have always wanted to help others and, many a time I have crossed the limits of *Fauj* (the Armed Forces). There was a civilian ward boy, in our hospital. His young wife was pregnant after about five or six years of marriage. She developed fever; diagnosed with malaria and was treated for the same. Owing to this complication, she delivered a premature baby boy at home who weighed just 1.50 kg. It was a severe winter that year. Our hospital did not have any incubators or paediatricians posted to take care of the child. With whatever help I could gather, and after stabilizing the child, I transferred the baby to the prestigious Christian Medical College Hospital at Ludhiana. The baby was refused admission and was sent back home. The parents were heartbroken. At this point, my team of nursing colleagues and I joined hands and decided to do our best. We explained the seriousness of the situation to the father of the child and told him we were trying our best to revive the baby. We turned innovative and fashioned a local incubator. It was a baby cradle padded on all the sides with blankets and cotton wool to provide insulation. The baby and mother were shifted to a small room, where no one was allowed other than the nurse on duty and myself, the doctor. The room was kept comfortably warm with heaters and blowers. The electricity would go off quite a few times. At those times, we used *sigris* (burners with coal) to keep the room warm and kept a constant watch for any carbon monoxide poisoning. We followed a strict dress code (sterilised clothes for the mother and the attending staff) and washed our hands meticulously to prevent any infections. The baby was fed mother's milk - the best food for a baby. As the baby was premature, he could not suckle. The mother expressed her milk and the nurse on duty fed the child slowly and carefully. Three nurses were on duty round the clock and no one could visit the mother and child. The baby gradually increased in weight and there was an overall improvement in his development. Our innovative incubator and Neonatal Intensive Care Unit (NICU) was home to the baby for nearly a month. When the baby left the hospital, we were all on cloud nine.

It was incredible because none of us had been trained for such an emergency, which even a reputed and better-equipped hospital had refused. We tackled it with our basic knowledge, sincerity, hard work and, of course, God Almighty's blessings. Very soon, the word spread, and we successfully handled two or three more such cases of premature babies. I published a paper on this subject in a medical journal. I was not a specialist then – I just had MBBS degree. However, thanks to my internship training, I was full of confidence in my ability to handle emergencies. During operations, my training had helped me to tackle many life-threatening emergencies. I had managed them with self-assurance and was able to save many lives and limbs. Sometimes, I did cross my limits. But my CO was very helpful, and he was always encouraging me once he realized the level of my sincerity to my profession and patients.

Drunken capers

The newspapers are brimming with stories of rats getting drunk in Bihar nowadays. I must narrate an unnatural occurrence which led to a very serious emergency. A detachment from another base moved to our base for some specific exercises. A few pilots, officers, a support team and *safaiwalas* formed the group. The officers had brought concentrated nitric acid to clean the toilets. Unfortunately, they had transported this in empty rum bottles. The *safaiwalas* were unaware that the rum bottles contained strong acid. When the officers were away at work, they decided to enjoy the 'high-quality rum' which the officers had hidden from them. They opened the bottles and gulped down the so-called rum. As a result, they were all writhing in severe pain and collapsed. It was a learning curve for all of us doctors in the unit – the process of treating them. We could not transfer them to a military hospital as the patients were not in a fit state, and they could have collapsed on the way. We could not initiate the usual treatments to revive them. A simple procedure, such as introducing a gastric tube, could lead to a tear or rupture of the stomach. The only thing we could do was to manage them conservatively and hope and pray that they'd recover. We fed them orally with milk, egg yolk, antacids and antibiotics and prayed like hell that they would retain the same. It took us almost a week to stabilise them. All of them recovered with God's grace. Later, they were transferred to a super speciality military hospital for further treatment of the complications that had set in. Small mistakes can lead to very big disasters.

By now, my duties were as Commanding Officer(CO) of the hospital (DSSC qualified), Senior Medical Officer (SMO) of the base (the senior-most doctor) and Squadron Medical Officer (aviation medicine qualified). And, of course, I was the adored LMO.

Life comes a full circle

Have you ever heard of *"Dava, Daru,* Parade"? Today as a veteran, I was waiting to collect my medicines. Once I had collected them, I rushed to the canteen to collect some groceries. Suddenly, I remembered the joke of *"dava daru parade"*. The ex-servicemen (veterans of the present day) queue up for their sick parade. In the services, reporting to the doctor for treatment when you are sick is also called a parade – 'sick parade'. Most of them were quite healthy. But they wanted to boast about their exploits in the various wars they had either participated in or were in service at that point of time. They would recall their heroic deeds, some actual and some imaginary, like the Burma operations or the Korean War, with great gusto - and finally, collect a few tablets. I used to wonder why they were wasting our time. Today as I was collecting the groceries I realized that I was doing the same, (*dava* means medicines and *daru* means liquor) buying groceries at the Canteen Stores Department (CSD) colloquially known as canteen. The *ex-servicemen* used to collect their quota of rum. How carefully they handled the bottles, caressing them fondly as if the bottles were their babies. It was a sight to be photographed and published in 'Time Magazine'! What you laughed at some years ago, you end up repeating, without you even being aware of it. Life comes full circle. That is life.

I would like to add my observations on today's internships. Following rigorous internship, a fresh medical graduate hones his/ her skill to tackle emergencies. A good MBBS doctor is the cry of the day in India. I believe internship has become an eyewash. Today's interns are studying for their MD/MS selection during internship and they have no time to learn and practice basic medical skills to save a patient. When do they learn basic clinical care?

After my retirement, I was in the panel at UPSC to select doctors. All those who reported were at least MD/MS, but they lacked basic skills, which was shocking. Internship is a very important part of the training process to become a good doctor. In our country, where people are going to quacks because of lack of medical facilities, a good, well-trained, motivated and empathetic doctor can play a vital role in providing quality medical care. Doctors should take internship seriously. There is plenty of time to prepare for their future dreams. Postgraduate studies can be done side by side during internship.

As a junior officer with hardly any experience, I could handle war emergencies. The credit goes to my teachers, my internship gurus and my faith in myself to do my best to help. I did succeed and thanks to that, they looked up to me as their beloved LMO.

The 1971 Operations

The Indo Pak war was looming large on the horizon. Our forward Air Force Station became a *non-family station*, which meant that other than the uniformed personnel, no one could stay. Our family, i.e. *babuji, ma* and our elder son, Amiya, who was then a few months old, were sent to Gwalior where my brother-in-law, Romanath was employed. He was married recently and, he and his wife, Sheela, a young graduate, were just beginning their married life at Gwalior.

Living in bunkers

My husband and I were stationed at our base. I lived with my medical team near the hospital in an underground bunker. My husband lived in another underground bunker in the technical area with his team. I was the only lady in the station at that time. Did I feel scared? Surprisingly, not at all. What a strange change in me. When I was a student in Pune, during the 1965 operations, I cried with fear for my parents and brothers as they were living in Delhi. Now, I was bang in the middle of the first strike airfield zone, but I did not feel scared. What do I owe my transformation to? I was trained to do my duties and this training helped tremendously. My staff did whatever they could to make me comfortable. This period of about six months, living in bunkers and sharing the same food, brought us close. We could share our problems, advise, console, sympathise with one another as in a family. This situation demanded a lot of discipline amongst us and built enduring friendships.

During operations, the food was served to us in the bunkers. We were issued enamel mugs to collect morning tea. The only concession the officer enjoyed was that he or she was the first one to be served. All of us had to carry our plates and enamel mugs if we wanted food and the steaming cup of tea. This reminded me of my AFMC days. All three meals were distributed at the respective bunkers. The food was good - wholesome, warm and tasty. There was not much variety, but I had no complaints and was satisfied. I was never a foodie and always enjoyed simple food. We were not allowed to leave our posts at any time. I was the only privileged one who could go home (the vacant family quarter) once a month to wash my hair.

In the thick of war

This was my first exposure to operations. I was excited that I would be able to do something for my country. I had joined AFMC to be of some use to my country. At the same time, I was worried about the safety of all Indians. I was reminded of the evergreen patriotic song sung by Bharat Ratna, Lata Mangeshkar, "*Jo laut ke ghar na aaye*". On December 3, 1971, there were air strikes in the early evening on all our forward airfields in the western sector, right from Amritsar to Agra. Soon after, our Honourable Prime Minister, Indira Gandhi declared that the war was 'ON', in the evening through All India Radio. The Pakistan Air Force attacked all our frontline air force stations. Our antiaircraft (ack ack) guns started roaring to take on the offending Pakistani aircraft. At that time, I saw the sky brightly lit up and heard the booming noise of the Anti-aircraft (ack-ack) guns. It looked like and reminded me of Diwali time. Immediately, everyone was ordered to go underground and take cover against the air attacks. We were cautioned to be ready for further air attacks and reminded to be ready to receive mass casualties at any time. Some of the runways (from where the aircrafts take off) were damaged partially because of Pakistani air strikes. They were repaired on the very same night with special materials. The first day of our offensive ops was heralded with the first rays of the sun. IAF fighter and bomber planes took off from all the airfields and pounded important targets in Pakistan like airfields, arsenal, fuel storage areas, trains loaded with arms, ammunition and personnel and many more. The war was 'ON'.

Our hospital was one of the first in the chain of evacuations from forward areas in the western sector. It was well equipped to carry out surgeries. In fact, many surgeries had been conducted here during the 1965 ops. Presently, there was no qualified surgeon/ anaesthetist posted in. The surgical team consisting of surgeons, orthopaedic surgeons, and anaesthetist was to arrive from Bangalore. This surgical team was to take over the trauma care and conduct the necessary life and limb-saving surgeries on the casualties and transfer them to specialised hospitals down the line for better care.

After the *strafing* of the previous evening, the enemy succeeded in aerial attacks of another nearby forward air base. There were many casualties on the very first day. The casualties arrived in all modes of transportation, from helicopters and cars to ambulances and tractors. There were about 200 of them. After *triage*, many were given first aid, including wound debridement, cleaning, disinfecting and suturing and sent back to their units to continue with the war efforts. Some, however, required urgent surgical intervention as their wounds had become infected and the infection was spreading very fast up the legs. I was scared, worried, confused and hoping against hope that the surgical team would arrive soon at the station. But, there was no news about the surgical team, which had left Bangalore well in time, much before the operations had started. However, they had not even reached Delhi by then. As a doctor, I could not fold my hands and just pray. I had to act fast to save the limbs and lives of my brother soldiers. I was in a great dilemma. On the one hand, the surgeons had not arrived. On the other hand, their condition was deteriorating every second. I took up the challenge to help my brother air warriors.

My training in the surgical division during internship helped me immensely. Amongst my staff, two air warriors were trained *Operation Room Assistants* (ORA). I managed the casualties conservatively with tetanus toxoid injections, heavy doses of antibiotics, excellent surgical care and in some cases, we even performed surgery. The ORAs were of great help and looked after the serious casualties round the clock. After stabilising the casualties, they were airlifted to the specialized centres. The not-so-serious were transferred by ambulance trains. This helped in saving their lives and improved the morale of the soldiers. In addition, this also helped to decongest the forward hospital so that we could receive the next wave of casualties. This boosted my self-confidence in tackling emergencies.

The air raid siren would start blaring at any time during the day or night, which meant the enemy aircrafts were overhead. Whatever was moving at that time, be it vehicles or humans, stopped at once. Those inside the vehicles quickly disembarked and slid under the vehicles in a jiffy for their safety and prayed like mad that the bomb was not targeted near their vehicle. This life-saving exercise was a routine drill for all of us.

The surgical team did finally arrive on the last day of operations. The operations had been called off with General Niazi's surrender at Dhaka. There was no direct route from Bangalore to Delhi in those days; one had to travel via Madras. The team had travelled in a military train which took a long time to reach its destination. The surgical team appreciated my work; they guided me in the handling of casualties who were being treated at the hospital and set course to Bangalore.

I must share another interesting episode. Our station commander allotted me a pistol for my self-defence. I tried to keep it between my petticoat and my body. It used to poke me all the time. I was very scared that it would fire accidentally and injure me or someone else. So, I went back to the Station Commander and asked him to take it back. I could not tell him the real reason but concocted a story, saying that I might pull the trigger if I really happened to encounter the enemy face to face. He understood the real cause of my problem and promptly asked me to change my uniform from saree to pant and shirt. This outfit was very comfortable and made it so much easier to slide under a vehicle, climb in and out of the bunkers and to get inside the fighter aircrafts to pull out injured pilots.

Local support

The local villagers aided and supported the armed forces wholeheartedly. Every day they would bring us homemade food, lot of sweets made of *asli ghee* (pure clarified butter) in huge baskets and vast quantities of dried fruits too. They were our biggest morale booster; their love and prayers for us inspired us always. As I was the only lady in the station, I was their heroine and they treated me like a Goddess. They felt very sorry for me as I'd had to send my baby away.

Hailed as heroes

During the time that we were busy with the operations, *babuji* fell sick and was in coma for nearly ten days soon after the war was declared. My youngest brother-in-law, Raghunath, had reached his side on his 'term break' from National Defence Academy (NDA) by their special train. We could not go as the war was raging in full blast. As soon as the operations ended, we were granted leave and we rushed to Gwalior. Our station commander was very compassionate, and we were the first to be granted leave. We travelled in the military coach in our *fatigues* (uniform). At every station, volunteers with food and refreshment packages would fill the air with rousing slogans such as *'Bharat mata ki jai', 'vande mataram', 'hamare veer jawanon badhe chalo',* etc. Milling crowds of local people would wait for hours for the military trains, to catch a glimpse of their heroes and heroines in uniform. They pampered us with goodies they had carried for us all the way from their villages. For me, it was the ultimate heaven to be a national idol! The love, affection and care our countrymen showered upon us cannot be described in words. After this wonderfully inspiring journey, we reached Gwalior.

As I have recounted earlier, b*abuji* recovered briefly from his coma on December 26, and gave us his final blessings before departing peacefully from his loved ones, the next day. He was only fifty-nine years old. He left us with cherished memories and a proud legacy to carry forward.

Setting a world record

Soon after, my husband and I were recommended by our Station Commander for the Presidential Award through the Air Force channel; and we were nominated for the Award of the 'Vishisht Seva Medal' together. This was a first in world history - a husband and wife receiving the Presidential Award at the same investiture parade at the same time. History was created. We were on cloud nine. I believe I must credit my Station Commander's belief in my professional capacity and my husband's constant help, guidance and support.

After the award, we were felicitated all over Punjab. I still remember the District Collector, Ludhiana, telling us that he could not allot land for the Presidential award to us as we were not from Punjab. But he said, he could allot us a plot of land if we paid a nominal sum. However, we did not have a few thousand of rupees to spare. We were not too concerned about getting land in Punjab. We enjoyed the hospitality, gorged on the rich food and soaked in the adulation and admiration. The beautiful shawls they presented to us were our trophies, something which was closest to our heart. We were young, naïve and not worldly-wise but we were happy with what we had. I have no regrets for not owning a plot at Civil Lines in Ludhiana. Contentment is essential for happiness in life.

From the wheat bowl of Punjab, we were posted to the sunny south - to the temple town of Madras (Air Force Avadi).

My other exposure to operations was during the Kargil war. The enemy had occupied the icy heights of Kargil with the sole aim of cutting off the Ladakh region. By this time, I had become a senior officer and was more involved in planning, manning, staffing, provisioning and executing and not in the actual war zone. Let me recall an interesting incident from this period. I had gone to inspect one of the forward airfields in Jammu & Kashmir (J&K) for their operational preparedness. After the usual socializing and dinner, I was alone in the VIP room in the officer's mess. The cook, who was all along present, was a tall middle-aged Kashmiri. He advised me to keep the door closed and not to open it till he came back the next morning. He also confirmed that all the doors were closed and bolted from inside. As he left, I closed the main door. I realized that the bedroom and the bathroom did not have any bolts to lock them. At about the same time, the lights went off and there was no emergency light or generator to take over. In the dark, I decided to wait in the drawing room for the lights to come on. Suddenly, I saw a silhouette and got frightened out of my wits. It was the cook; I had seen his shadow. He lit a candle for me. After regaining my composure, I asked him how he had got in. He showed me a gaping space in the kitchen, where the window should have been. On the very next day, the window was fixed, and bolts and latches were fixed in all the rooms. No lady had ever stayed in the VIP room till that day. This was quite an unnerving experience for me.

I cannot describe the details of many activities in their entirety owing to security concerns. If you work in an operational situation, you learn so much; you learn how to tide over in an emergency, you tap your potential and resources till the last squeeze. You need to improvise a lot to attain your goals and, most importantly, have a positive attitude. You should never give up under the most adverse circumstances.

In the end, the nation remembered the brave heroes who did not return. "They had promised they would come back soon... they more than kept their words. They went as men. They came back as heroes".

War is always stressful and traumatic, but it has its positive side too. In such times, you end up cultivating rewarding associations, lifelong friendships and indelible memories.

My First Post Graduation

We arrived in Bangalore from Madras (the previous station) for my advanced course at the Institute of Aviation Medicine (IAM), Bangalore in May/June 1974. Along with my husband and I, my elderly mother-in-law, my youngest brother-in-law and our four-year-old son accompanied us. We had only our clothes with us in our carry-on luggage. There were no vessels to cook with and no house to live in. We stayed in the mess for a few days. My husband had to go back to Avadi, Madras and later proceed on a course to Coimbatore. So, he left after a few days.

House Hunting

My youngest brother-in-law and I roamed around Bangalore house hunting. We used to start the day after breakfast in our proud 'Mercedes Benz', our Vespa scooter. We would spend the whole day roaming around various colonies where we had heard that houses were available for rent. In those days, there were no 'Magic bricks' or other websites to help us. However, in the first week, we had no luck. We had a constraint since we were looking for a house near my place of work so that commuting would be easier for me. After about a week, my brother-in-law's leave was almost up, and he had to go back to NDA. We both were physically and emotionally drained out. My brother-in-law went back to NDA when his leave finished. We had not found a house by then. The Officer's Mess asked me to vacate as we were not permitted to live in the mess beyond a certain period. My senior colleague from AFMC, who was also undergoing the course, offered his house as his family had not moved in yet. This was a god sent gift for me. We shifted into the house immediately. However, we had no bedding to sleep and no vessels to cook food.

Why did we have no bedding or vessels? When we left Avadi for Bangalore, the vehicle carrying the luggage broke down right in front of the railway station in Madras. The luggage arrived in bits and pieces from Madras to Bangalore whenever there was space available in the goods train. Every day, I visited the station to collect the luggage. If the luggage was not collected on time, the railways levied *demurrage* charges.

On the family front
Abortion attempt

On the home front, I was all alone, somehow managing my elder son and my ailing, old mother-in-law. Professionally, I was a student officer. To add to all this chaos, I was not keeping well because of the early pregnancy. I was expected to deliver around the middle of March, which was also the time for my university examination. There was no one to talk to or consult. In that dire situation, I decided to get my pregnancy terminated. Thank God! I did not go ahead. And now, I am the mother of a wonderful son - Ajit Banerjee. It was a blessing in disguise that the doctor was worse than a butcher and I escaped.

Meera's arrival

My only sister-in-law arrived with her two sons around the same time as I was grappling with professional studies, my personal life and various other issues. She was expecting her third child, and she was around three to four months pregnant. Her two sons were very good looking and were real darlings. The children were perpetually hungry. In those days, I used to cook and then proceed to the office. I am not exaggerating - I used to make around 60-65 *parathas*(homemade wheat pancake) and a dozen boiled eggs and some vegetable and then will proceed for my classes. I used to spend another two hours studying in the library and would get back home around 5 pm. As I would wheel the scooter inside the gate, all the three kids which include our son too, would come running to me crying, "Mami/ Mamma, we are hungry." I was at the end of my tether and found it hard to be patient. I was not keeping well. I was suffering from early stages of *Toxemia of Pregnancy,* a complication of pregnancy. In short,

I was bloating, and my blood pressure was hitting the roof. At the sight of three hungry kids, I would quietly go to the kitchen and make a quick *khichdi* or some other concoction so that the kids could eat. Meera delivered a healthy boy and left for her home with her three sons.

Being a post-graduate student

From mother, expectant mother to a PG student, I had to change like a chameleon. This was my first postgraduate course. You may wonder why I am making such a big deal of a post-graduate course? It is because I successfully completed many PG courses later. But, I found this diploma course a huge challenge. When I was offered MD Pediatrics a few years earlier, I could not take it up, because I was newly married, getting used to and learning the family culture and most importantly, our elder son was on his way. Later, to attain the much-coveted MD degree, I had to touch my nose in a circuitous way, going around my ears. Despite my postgraduate diplomas and degrees, I could not become a medical specialist and a cardiologist, which was my dream and I was capable of. Many facets of life are beyond one's control. The lesson is: "Do not give up and excel in whatever you are doing." That is what I did which propelled me to become "the lady with many firsts".

The first lady

I was the first lady student at the institution. It was a great dilemma for my teachers and me. They had never had a lady student undergoing the advanced course in Aviation Medicine till that day. The subject is very different from what I expected. Aviation medicine is mainly applied physiology, but there is a lot of applied physics, high-altitude physiology, acceleration physiology, ejection from the aircraft, space physiology, biochemistry, vibration and many other subjects. Medicine as applicable to the aircrew was covered in detail. There is a lot of experimental and practical work. *Anthropometry* was an important tool to design and make the best flying clothing for the aircrew, like *anti G suits, partial and full pressure suits.* All this was new to me. The student and the teachers were having a tough time. One of my senior instructors used to joke with me. He used to say, "Why have you come here? To become a tailor or a cobbler?" However, I persisted and did quite well. That was how I became the first lady aviation medicine specialist in Southeast East Asia.

Examination

My examination and delivery date were fast approaching. My mother came to help us to tide over the crisis. After attending classes, I used to be dead tired and would return home and lie down. Jayant, my friend philosopher and guide would read out the important portions for the examination from the living room while I was resting in the bedroom. It seems unbelievable that a colleague could help me so much, especially when I was his competitor! I can never forget all the help Jayant extended to me.

During one of the monthly examinations, I did not know the answers to any of the questions. There was no invigilator in the room. I was sitting and staring at the roof. The professor walked in and asked me why I was not writing the paper? I replied that I did not know the answers. He was impressed by my sincerity and integrity and told me that I could set my own questions and answer them. I did. It's rare to see such teachers, who believed their students, and students who lived up to the expectations of their teachers. Contrast that with today's parents scaling tall buildings to help their children and the children willing to employ any and every wrongful means to score marks.

At the fag end of the course, I weighed 82 kg; my feet were like inflated tyres and I could not fit into any shoes. So, I was excused from wearing shoes on medical grounds and allowed to wear slippers. In the Armed Forces, shoes are an integral part of the uniform and one must wear them always unless specifically excused. I used to feel giddy very often and used to black out at times. By then, maternity leave was authorised for lady doctors in Armed Forces and I was on maternity leave for two months. Sadly, however, the course was in its final phase and my university examination was fast approaching. So, I was still attending the Institute while on maternity leave.

Chatterjee Sir

After I qualified for my theory examination, I was posted at the Department of High Altitude Physiology, IAM for thesis work under the guidance of then Wing Commander PC Chatterjee. It is difficult to get a guide of such high integrity, moral values and someone so fearless. While the other guides were helping their students to write the thesis, my guide was making me learn how to weld electric wires. The practical did not commence till almost the last two months. Once, I asked him why I was learning to weld. He answered that every aspect had to be learnt and I should not depend on anyone for any help for my thesis. That was a lesson which I tried to emulate throughout my life.

Colonel Sir

This was quite a funny episode. One day, 'Colonel (Col) Sir' reported for his review medical and fitness for promotion following a heart ailment. It was my job to evaluate him in the high-altitude chamber as per protocol, I explained the procedure and requested him to get into the altitude chamber. He looked at me and the chamber in turn for quite some time. I was puzzled and started wondering whether I had made some mistakes. Suddenly, Col Sir exclaimed, "Will the chamber break the roof and fly to high altitude?" At first, I did not understand. When his query sunk in, I realized his fear. We, at IAM are so used to various chambers. Others don't understand as to how while sitting inside a chamber at ground level, they are being exposed to an altitude of 15,000 feet, They, wonder how they are going to reach that altitude. I explained that the chamber does not fly physically, but air from the chamber is evacuated through a vacuum pump to reach specific altitudes and he was satisfied. I could complete his run without any glitches.

My delivery

When I developed labour pains, I reported to the hospital. The obstetrician examined me and decided that I needed a C section but finally I had a normal delivery and my second son, Ajit was born. I have gone into the details of my delivery in one of the following chapters.

'God helps those who help themselves'. This quote really helped me. Instead of wallowing in self-pity, I took up Aviation Medicine and contributed my bit. Our younger son is a darling and is the pride of the whole Banerjee family. Both my aims were achieved because of God Almighty's blessings, my husband's constant support and my hard work.

The Good, the Bad & the Ugly of 'Athithi'

New security officer

Athithis (guests) are considered as God incarnate in our culture. An *athithi* is meant to be looked after with love and respect. In the *Tirukkural* (a text of everyday virtues) there is a couplet, I quote: "Moppakkuzhaium anicham, mugam thirindu nokkakuzhaium virindu" Translated from Tamil, it means, if you smell the flower known as *Anicham,* it will wilt. The guest will wilt if he sees your unhappy face from a distance. Today, this sort of hospitality is not possible and we wait for the *athithi* to depart at the earliest. Now it is *"ahtithi tum kab jaoge"*!

In this chapter, I am going to talk about some of my experiences with *athithis*. This is not an exhaustive list of experiences. There are so many more that I cannot recall.

Shortly after I was married, I was posted out to a forward airfield in Punjab but my husband was not posted with me. *Ma* and *Babuji* accompanied me and were with me for the first few months - 'to take care of me' in the absence of my husband. He was at his *karmabhoomi* in Bengaluru. My in-laws wanted to spend some time at their home in Meerut. I came back home alone after settling them at Meerut. I was sad to enter an empty house without my in-laws. When I arrived back at my unit, I was welcomed with the fantastic news of my husband's posting to the same place where I was posted. My happiness knew no bounds. To add to my joy, my youngest brother-in-law, who had passed his *matric* from the UP Board, Meerut, was to join the local college near our Air Force Station for his Intermediate. A few days later, the three of us were living in our 'palatial' house which had three bedrooms and a kitchen.

A friend I'll never forget

The months flew with all three of us busy with our own schedules. We enjoyed being together. A new security officer was posted in from a*non-family station* - meaning, his family was not allowed to stay with the officer in his previous station. His family, consisting of his wife and two children - one daughter aged five and a son aged two - were staying in Kanpur. He put in a request for sharing accommodation with us. There were only three of us and the house had three huge rooms. We wanted to help the senior officer as he was arriving from a field area and I have no regrets about doing so. I think those were the best days of our life at that place. What *bhabhiji* (the wife of the senior officer) did for us is something I can never forget till my dying day. She was a tall, graceful *sardarni* (Sikh woman), very pious and loving.

All three of us and her husband left for our respective workplaces around 7 am. At that time, my husband used to come home anytime after 5 pm and her husband too would get back around the same time; my youngest brother-in-law would return around 3 pm after his college got over and I would return as soon as the patients were all attended to, at indefinite hours. I was in the early stages of my pregnancy. *Bhabhiji* would make some of the tastiest food I've ever eaten and would wait for each one of us. On our arrival, she would make steaming hot *phulkas (rotis)* for each one of us and would wait till we finished our food. She used to pray for nearly one hour, reading the "Guru Granth Sahib" and would ride her husband's Royal Enfield for fun in the evenings in those days. She cooked delicious food every day, fed each one of us with love and affection, looked after her children and looked after me as my mother would. She came from a very affluent background, but was very humble and down to earth. It is hard to believe that such good people exist. After about three months, they were allotted their own accommodation. We continued to visit them and have dinner together daily for nearly a month. Their son would not eat his food till we reached their place. I learnt the true meaning of sharing, caring and love from her. They were very grateful to us for sharing our house with them. We, in turn, were always indebted to them for the love and affection they showered on us and, of course, the fantastic food she fed us every day.

An unwanted guest

My husband and his *masima* (aunt) along with our elder son were going to meet *masima's* spiritual guru. He met with a scooter accident on the way and broke his left-hand bone (Radius). The accident took place in a civil area. Our elder son, who was about four years old then, ran around asking for help. Luckily for us, one of my husband's friends lived there and he took him to the Air Force hospital. We had called one of his old course-mate for dinner that day as his wife was away. As soon as I heard the news, I rushed to the hospital, arranged for my husband's surgery and brought *masima* and my son back home. The scooter was at the police station.

The gentleman arrived for dinner in the evening. I explained the situation to him, hoping that he would leave. But no, he settled down comfortably for dinner. I assumed he would leave after dinner. That didn't happen either! He declared that he would spend the night at our place and regally handed over a written list of what he required immediately after he woke up and his breakfast preferences! And amazingly, he did not even bother to enquire about my husband, his friend who had invited him. Rather, he was feeling bad that no liquor was offered during dinner since I had made it amply clear that I do not touch liquor and no liquor would be served when my husband was away. I was fuming inside and wanted him to GET OUT. The next morning, I organised whatever he had asked for and left a note asking him to leave as soon as possible as I would be spending the whole day at the hospital with my husband. I never saw him again in my life. Here was a case of a selfish a*thithi* with no empathy.

Anthony amma

With two children, an ailing, old mother-in-law and both of us holding full-time jobs in the Air Force, it was becoming difficult for us to manage all the fronts. Full-time help became a necessity and not a luxury anymore. Through the government department of Women and Child Welfare, Karnataka, we employed Anthony Amma, along with her baby boy, Anthony. She was a Christian by birth; had fallen in love with a Hindu boy and had become an unwed mother. She went to her church which gave her shelter till her delivery. However, the church could not keep her and her baby boy as it was against their rules. Our younger son and Anthony were practically the same age.

She was a very nice, hardworking, simple, accommodative young girl and she slept at the top of the staircase. The child, of course, was with her all the time. The two babies were growing up together. One day, the house was being whitewashed. All the household items were outside and inside the house was a mess. We asked Anthony amma to take the children out so that they wouldn't get dirty. Her son's complexion was on the darker side, our elder boy was brown and our younger son was fair by Indian standards. There was an old guitar lying at home which was kept outside. She took the guitar and the three kids. She carried the two babies and was playing the guitar and singing with our elder son, god knows how! It was a sight to watch. People took her to be a beggar and even offered her money. In the meantime, the police spotted her and thought she was absconding with the kids. They huddled them all into their van and brought them home. They got our address from our elder son who could speak a few basic sentences in English at that time. We were wonderstruck: why had the police come and that too with our children? When we heard the story, we burst out laughing and of course thanked the police for bringing the children back home. We acknowledged that she was our helper and that we had asked her to take the children out for some time.

The lady who refused to leave

A third baby boy joined the gang soon after this incident. My sister-in-law, Meera befriended a Naval Officer's wife while she was admitted at hospital for her delivery. This lady was highly qualified (M Tech) and was employed as a scientist in one of the national laboratories in Bangalore. She was admitted in the same room as Meera and possibly had some *gynaecological* problem. Later, being from the services, we became friends.

A few months later, her husband was posted out to another naval station. She was living with her helper, an elderly lady, in a rented house. We used to look her up as she was a brother officer's wife. She delivered a baby boy around the same time as our younger son was born. Gradually, she started complaining that the landlord was troubling her. One day she arrived at our house, unheralded, with her bag and baggage, her son and her helper. We had just two bedrooms and the house was already overcrowded. When she arrived at our house, she said she would find accommodation in a few days and move out. Those 'few days' extended to nearly six months.

We gave her the second room. She did not contribute even a wee bit to the household chores. Poor Anthony amma used to take care of cooking, cleaning and washing clothes for all of us. If I ever did ask her to help, the lady would say, "I am a highly qualified lady and I do not know household work." She would order for her favourite dishes daily, (mostly non-vegetarian). I used to procure the items from the market and Anthony amma would cook specially for her. This went on. The worst was that she would buy chocolates or candy for her son only. She would never give a single piece to the other two babies. I just could not tolerate her. But I did not know how to throw her out. Even her helper would do nothing except look after her baby. I offered to search for a house for her. She came up with the excuse of not having utensils to cook food. I offered her utensils free of cost, but she still refused to move. In all this melee, we tried to contact her husband but all our attempts failed. He never came back to look them up in those six months, nor did 'she' ever offer to share the household expenses.

Finally, I had a eureka moment! The idea that clicked was a hilarious one. This *athithi* was very fond of non-vegetarian food. So, we told her that my parents were coming and that no non-vegetarian food would be cooked at home. Presto, as soon as she heard the news, she left the house without even bothering to inform us about her departure. I still do not know where she went but we managed to get rid of her. I learnt a valuable lesson - never allow anyone into your house without knowing their background.

A clash of cultures

Traditionally, the *Upanayanam* in Sanskrit or *Poite* in Bengali and *Poonal* in Tamil is a very important religious function for boys. It is also known as the thread ceremony. My mother-in-law insisted that this function be performed on a grand scale, almost like a marriage, even though my husband and I were not keen on it. My sons are the only two grandsons in the family. *Ma* was the eldest amongst seven sisters and five brothers. There were representatives from each of her brothers' and sisters' families for the function. In total, at least 60 people had come from *Ma's* side. My parents and my brothers-in-law and their families had also come. It was a huge crowd. My husband had never wanted to call the whole family. He knew very well that it would be difficult to keep everyone happy, or at least satisfied, with the resources we could muster.

All the relatives arrived one by one and were settled in our house and another house we had hired nearby. A cook was employed and all the food was served under one roof. On the day of the function everything went off well. For the second time, I was going to face cultural differences boomeranging into a war of sorts. This time, the stakes were high as there was such a large number of relatives, each with their individual preferences. Amongst south Indians, the thread ceremony is a very sacred function and non-vegetarian food is a complete no-no. My *Ma's* brothers and sisters being from the renascent east, believed that food without fish and meat was not fit for the consumption of the *bhadralok*. Usually, at our home, except for myself, we did partake non-vegetarian dishes. However, when my parents were at home, it was avoided as a mark of respect to their feelings.

After the function, we expected the relatives to leave one after the other. But, they had different plans. They had come to South India with a plan of touring and visiting important places. Attending the function was just an excuse. After the first day of strict vegetarian food, they wanted to have non-vegetarian food to be cooked and served at home. My mother almost collapsed on hearing the demand for fish. It was a task for me to control my youngest brother-in-law, the proverbial hot-tempered *Laxman* of the family, who was deeply attached to us and wanted to confront all his *masis* and *mamas* immediately.

How were we to find a solution? *Athithi Devo Bhava* – 'the guests' wish is our primary duty'. My husband had anticipated a situation like this. Both of us ran around searching for a small apartment for a few days for my parents to stay. Finally, we found a garage with an attached toilet. We shifted them there the same evening. We visited them every day taking meals for them in a *tiffin* box. It was a culture shock to them as they had never had non-vegetarian food at home.

At home, I faced a lot of criticism for not looking after the guests properly. The food problem was sorted out after my parents moved out. But there was a water problem too. Water used to be available only for a few hours in the morning. None of our guests would get up early and get ready when there was water supply. Their day would start only after the water supply had stopped for the day. We had to buy water to provide for our guests.

In today's busy world where nuclear families have become the norm, it is becoming more and more challenging to look after the guests. It's *okay* if they come for a meal. Otherwise, with both husband and wife working and household help in short supply, it becomes tough to have house guests. These days, guests are usually entertained in clubs, restaurants or hotels as per one's choice and means. As women are working full time, it gives them a respite. But, when your own family members arrive for family functions, you can't be entertaining them at hotels.

If you are a guest at someone's house, please remember the opening line of this chapter. Look at the constraints and help your hosts as much as possible. Plan to move out as early as possible, instead of parking yourself in someone's home for a long time. Get welcomed as *'Athithi Devo Bhava'* and not as *'Athithi tum kab jaoge'*.

The Invincible Ajit

Along with progress in my advanced course, I realized that I was also getting along with my second pregnancy. I was not keeping well throughout my second pregnancy.

Scooter accident

My friend, philosopher and guide, then Flt Lt Jayant Kulkarni and now Maj General J S Kulkarni (Retired), is one of the most intelligent, empathetic and kind-hearted people. I have always valued his friendship. He helped everyone in need. He helped me at every step of my service career. It is a blessing to have a friend like Jayant. Despite my husband and I being *gazetted officers*, all we possessed was a scooter and a bicycle. At this juncture, we were building a house at Jalahalli in Bangalore. As my pregnancy advanced, I could not drive the scooter anymore. So, Jayant and I pooled our two-wheelers. The day Jayant drove our scooter, my husband would cycle to the office. On one such occasion, we were late to the Institute. Our boss, Air Commodore JHF Manekshaw, the elder brother of India's first five-star General, was a stickler for time and discipline. To beat the time element, Jayant was driving very fast and I was sitting pillion. Suddenly, I felt an impact and everything went dark. I could not fathom what had gone wrong. Then, it was all bright and I found my husband standing there with a worried face. He was happy to see me alive and smiling. What was the mystery? Since we were late, Jayant was driving at breakneck speed. Suddenly a *three-tonner* (military truck) emerged from the only gate, which was both the 'in' gate and 'out' gate. It was exiting our unit premises to drop air warriors to other units. A head-on collision took place and both of us were thrown under the three-tonner, which was why it was suddenly dark. After the commotion, the three-tonner moved a little and we both emerged smiling. My unborn child was safe. It was God's will that we were safe. My husband was relieved to see me. Even before Jayant and I had discovered what had gone wrong, information had reached my husband's unit that I was under a three-tonner following a direct collision. He was really worried about both of us. Every cloud has a silver lining and thanks to this accident, the other gate, the 'exit gate' which was always kept closed was now opened.

Roasted in the hot cockpit

The Director of Aeronautics visited our institute. The boss did not know where to hide this little elephant – full-term pregnant lady weighing 82 Kgs, i.e. me! After lengthy discussions and deliberations, it was decided that I would be the experimental subject in the *hot cockpit*. Director Aeronautics would be demonstrated the effects of extreme heat on our pilots and the various means developed to ameliorate the heat stress would be explained to him. Director Aeronautics could not see me, except my face. For me, it was torture being exposed to those high temperatures for about two hours.

My delivery

After a day or two of this exposure, I developed labour pains and reported to the hospital. The obstetrician examined me and decided that I needed a 'C' section because of my *toxaemia*. She asked the Junior Resident to prepare me for a C section. After she left, I requested the junior resident to give me some tranquillizers so that I could sleep for some time. I told him that once I had rested, he could prepare me for the C Section. He obliged. When I woke up after a sound sleep, I was refreshed. I was listening to the radio commentary of a hockey match. As Ajit Pal Singh, the captain, scored the winning goal, our younger son was born. He was named Ajit after the captain. The senior arrived on the scene and was about to scold the junior resident for not preparing me for a caesarean. She stopped herself on hearing the healthy cry of a lovely baby.

I was very keen on a normal delivery. Otherwise, I could not have appeared for my examinations, which were due to start in a few days after my delivery. If I had to drop out or fail, that would mean curtains on my post-graduation throughout my service career. Owing to the clinical condition I was in, a normal delivery seemed impossible, but ultimately happened, by God's will. While the newborn was being attended to by my mother in the hospital, I appeared for my Post-Graduate(PG) examination. I returned home from the hospital after successfully clearing the PG Diploma examination and with our younger son.

Ajit - Lord Krishna

Our son, Ajit was like Lord Krishna. He faced innumerable obstacles during pregnancy. His own stupid mother had wanted to abort him because she wanted to be a post-graduate. This was followed by a direct collision during the advanced stages of pregnancy and being roasted in a hot cockpit on the previous day of delivery. Normal delivery was nigh impossible thanks to my health conditions at that time. All these only go to substantiate the saying, *'jaake rake saiya, maar sake na koy'*, meaning 'if God wants you to be alive and kicking, no harm will ever come to you'. If God wills, nothing is impossible.

A second hurdle

My next hurdle was to complete a research project within six months; If I completed thesis successfully, only then I would be eligible for the PG Diploma. My routine continued as before but now there was a newborn baby to look after. The minute I changed into uniform, he would start howling. We still had Amiya's old perambulator with half-broken wheels. It was like a family heirloom! My parents had tied a medium-sized rope on to it; they would place Ajit inside and pull it along since the pram could not move on its own. Once this party - comprising my parents, a broken and screeching pram and my baby – left, I used to leave for duty. They would stop at the corner of the road. When my parents observed that I had left, they would pull the pram back home. This was a daily routine. My mother used to carry a bottle of milk hidden under her saree. My little son would somehow extricate the milk bottle and drink up the milk.

However, it was not easy for me. I could cheat the child and leave home. But, what about my motherly instincts? After delivery, a woman's hormones are working overtime. My blouses used to be drenched every two to three hours. I used to feel miserable, not because my uniform was a mess but for my son, who was not getting proper nutrition because his mother was absorbed in her studies. I always carried an extra uniform blouse to change into. There's a lesson in life for all of us. It is not easy to achieve anything. There will always be obstacles. The worst of them all is self-guilt. I had to work very hard to get over my guilt and it took me a very long time.

Was it fate or a cruel joke?

When I was offered an MD, post-graduate degree course on a platter, right after my MBBS, I did not take up the offer because I wanted to be an ideal mother and devote myself to bringing up our first child. The wheels of time had taken a full circle and now I was running helter-skelter to be admitted for post-graduation. Finally, I was admitted for a post-graduate diploma. This time, my poor child was under the care of my parents. Even today, I am overcome by guilt when I remember those days. It was very tough for the child, but emotionally, it was traumatic for me.

Colourful tablets

Our younger son was growing up well and our elder son's birthday was fast approaching. We had asked our elder son to clean the mantelpiece and decorate the living room for the party. In his enthusiasm, he cleaned it very well. However, in the process, some of Ma's medicines had fallen onto the ground. The younger one at that stage was crawling and trying to stand up and used to put everything in his mouth. I was busy in the office because of my thesis work and during the evenings, there were a lot of parties to attend as many officers were posted in and out from both our units. Attending these parties was compulsory. In between, whenever I enquired about how the child was, *Ma* would reply that he was fine. After two days, when the child was in a deep sleep, I asked my *Ma* whether he had drunk his milk. That was when she told me that for the past two days, he had not had any milk, and all he was doing was sleeping. I went into panic mode as I realized that the child was in a coma. Immediately, we took the child to the paediatrician at the hospital; he did a stomach wash and revived the child. But he gave me more than a mouthful for my negligence. I deserved that and much more.

What happened?

To date, we do not know what happened. We presume that he might have picked up and eaten the attractive coloured tablets that could have fallen on the floor. I am not sure what exactly happened. But the result was that the child went into a coma.

Negligent mother

As a mother, I failed to perform my duties appropriately. As a human being, you have a certain amount of time and energy and, with my studies, I had been using up every ounce of my energy. The problem was that my innocent little younger son had become last priority in my daily routine since *Ma* was supposed to be looking after him. I learnt a harsh lesson: "do not neglect your toddlers or for that matter your children at any stage" because of various pressures that may assume more importance. Nothing is more important than your child. Thankfully, Ajit - the invincible - faced a life-threatening situation and emerged victoriously. I am narrating this story in detail to emphasise this lesson to all new mothers. Working mothers also have dreams to climb up the career ladder. There is nothing wrong in that; I do believe that one must aspire to do better in their chosen career. But, please remember, if you have a child, they need your time also and at times, on a priority basis. Please do not ignore them. I learnt my lesson the hard way. Children are like young saplings. They need all our attention, love and care in addition to the soil (the home environment) and manure (food) we provide. Only then will the plant (child) grow well and face the world, with all its good and bad, confidently.

Bhindi dada

Our neighbour, Mr. Chakravarty, had a similar background to ours; he was a Bengali married to a Punjabi and had two sons. Our elder son and their younger son, Bunty used to play together. When Ajit was about six months old, Amiya would carry him to the playground. Naturally, no one would play with such a small child. Amiya, however, would insist that unless Ajit could join in, he would not play. To be able to play with Amiya, the others would allow Ajit to play. He used to sit there and babble all the time, all the while enjoying the game. In between all this, the senior kids including Bunty would come there and play with Ajit for some time. Ajit could not pronounce his name properly and used to call him *bhindi dada.* We all used to laugh heartily whenever he called out *'bhindi dada'*. Even the youngster enjoyed the joke.

Junior Commander Course(**JCC**)

I passed the entrance examination and was selected for the Staff College course. I had to undergo a Junior Commander's Course at Coimbatore; it was a mandatory requirement. Ajit was about a year and a half while Amiya was six and a half years old. Amiya was attending school by then. Perforce, I had to leave Amiya behind. I took Ajit and a lady helper with me to Coimbatore. During the morning parade, he used to copy the way I marched during the parade and then my PT exercises. Thanks to his mimicry, I was kept entertained every evening. Soon after, we were posted to the Defence Services Staff College in Wellington, Ooty. The kids enjoyed the beauty of bountiful nature. At that time, Ajit was still very young and could not pronounce words clearly. Staff college was 'top college' for him. I knitted the famous 'top college' sweater for him which he flaunted amongst his friends.

Not knowing English

We never spoke English at home to inculcate the habit of speaking the mother tongue among our kids. Ajit's mother tongue was Bengali. Most of the kids of his age could manage some spoken English and that became the cause of discrimination. They refused to play with him. He used to come back home crying, "Mamma, they do not play with me because I cannot speak proper English." I used to console him, telling him that he would learn proper English very soon. And he did. Today, he is settled in USA and of course, speaks fluent English. In addition, I am proud to say that he can speak Hindi, Bengali, Tamil and French quite well.

Talented children

Both the kids were exceptionally good in studies as well as sports. We are truly blessed parents. Whenever his teacher awarded 'Good' or 'Very Good', Ajit would come running to us to countersign the notebook. When he scored 100% marks in his tests, he would ask me to sign on the answer paper which had to be returned to the school. We had to sign with our official designation. If we signed Baba/Mamma, he used to get upset. I had to sign as P Bandopadhyay, Sqn Leader, SMO, or CO, 9AFH. Then, he would be happy and used to show off to his classmates. Of course, we had to celebrate with his favourite biscuits. There is an advertisement which shows a mother rewarding her daughter with chocolate as the child had scored very good marks. Every child needs reinforcement in some form – it could be biscuits, chocolates, a pat on the back or even a good word. Ajit was also very good in recitation. He recited *Jhansi ki Rani* when the chief of the French Air Force visited our station. The French chief could not understand the poem but comprehended the gist of it thanks to Ajit's recitation and the actions accompanying it. He was thoroughly impressed. His recitation was the talk of the station for many years. My husband had trained both the children. We were very proud of them and in return, both the boys were very proud of their parents.

Indian Institute of Technology (IIT)

Thanks to his hard work and talent, Ajit qualified for Indian Institute of Technology (IIT). On the day the results were announced, he went to IIT Delhi to check whether he had passed the entrance examination. We were waiting at home to know the results. There was no news. Finally, one of his friends informed us that he had cleared the admission process with a very good rank. My first reaction was to pay my thanks to God Almighty. My father and I went to a nearby temple and prayed. My father was living with my brother in Delhi at that time. When I heard the good news, I had bought broiler chicken, which was Ajit's favourite. After the temple visit, my father insisted on coming home to congratulate him. What could I do with the chicken? Well, it went straight down the drain! Ajit was miserable when he heard about the incident later. Anyway, he joined IIT Kanpur which was Number One in those days.

Life at Kanpur

I am sure Ajit enjoyed the academics at IIT. He enjoyed his freedom and loved eating *dhaba* food, which is tasty but unhealthy. He was transferred from Kanpur to Delhi because he contracted severe jaundice. He had turned yellow like turmeric; he could not eat, and if he ate, he would instantly vomit. As a result, he became skin and bone and weighed just 36 kg, for a height of nearly 6 feet. He was admitted to hospital and his father stayed by his side throughout his hospital stay; he would feed him small quantities of food and entertain him with stories.

His father would physically carry him like one would a baby. It was a tough period, and we both were very scared of the outcome. After about a month and a half, he improved slightly and insisted on going back to college. Promptly, he was back at the hospital with severe typhoid, which kept him in the hospital for another six weeks. His father looked after him and hardly ate or slept. Finally, the poor boy recovered; however, he could not appear for his first semester examinations. For the remaining four years of his course, he could not come home during the holidays as he had to clear paper after paper from the first term. He passed the finals with very good scores and managed to do so without losing a single term. He learnt an important lesson in food hygiene and never ate from roadside food stalls after that. "Swachh Bharat" had not caught on as a concept then.

Going to USA

Soon after passing out of IIT, Ajit worked at the Supercomputer Centre in Bangalore for a few months. He joined one of the prestigious colleges in Pennsylvania for his MTech. He went on a scholarship and was also allowed to teach the undergraduates. Today, he is happily settled in USA.

A 60ᵗʰ birthday cruise

We used to visit Ajit every year and enjoyed with him, and later with his wife and now his son, Sanjay. They are a happy family who spread joy to all those around them. I have to say once again how proud I am of both our sons. He arranged for a 19-day Alaskan Cruise as a gift on our 60th birthday. What a wonderful gift! We both enjoyed ourselves thoroughly. I remember this funny incident. On the very first day, I noticed a red light flashing from a telephone-like structure. Since we both are from the armed forces, the one thing we both are trained to recognise is that 'RED' means danger. We Indians as a rule have a habit of asking others and not reading and finding out for ourselves – the *bhai saab* concept. When the red light flashed, instead of reading the instruction manual, I nagged my husband to go and find out what the emergency was. Initially, he did not oblige but when my nagging increased along with my decibel levels, he had no choice but to go. He went to the control room of the cruise ship, which is right at the bottom. People working there were aghast on seeing him there and angry as it was a 'NO TRESPASS ZONE'. When he explained why he had come, one of them came up with him. By this time, the flashing red light had disappeared. What was the emergency? The fellow opened the instruction manual and read out loud. And what did he read?

There was a phone call for us. The phone call was from Ajit. The crew member shot us a dirty look and left. We did feel bad but laughed our guts out at our stupidity.

Ajit calls up every Sunday on Skype and we chat for almost an hour or so. My grandson teaches me French and I teach him Hindi, Bengali and Tamil. My daughter-in-law is an affectionate lady and looks after us very well when we visit them. They visit India too and she specifically enjoys the cultural diversity of the country. May God grant them happiness, peace, success and contentment in their lives.

God Almighty blessed us with two wonderful boys, their lovely wives (who are so affectionate) and our three musketeers (grandsons), who are the reason for our living.

Officer...Lady Officer

I appeared for the Defence Services Staff College (DSSC) exam along with my husband. Both of us felt that we could get a chance for a posting together after the Staff College course. When I reported at the examination centre, all the other officers assumed that I was the official invigilator till the question paper was distributed. It was only then that they realized that I too was competing in the exam.

Initially, I decided not to join the DSSC. My previous Station Commander, who was by then Air Officer Commanding-in-Chief (AOC-in-C), advised us that I should attend the course as I had qualified and been selected in my branch. It would be an honour to the Indian Air Force (IAF) as I would be the first service lady officer (The lady in blue) to undergo the course.

Reception at Mettupalayam

At the staff college, the houses are allotted to you as per the size of your family and not as per seniority, which is an exception. I moved in with our two sons, my parents who accompanied me to look after the kids, our two dogs and a domestic help. My husband made me write, "husband on weekends". My very big family was allotted No 1, Nilgiri right next to the Officer's Mess, which had a telephone. This was the house closest to the college. I still did not know how to drive a car. And now, driving would be even more difficult, as it was tough to drive in the hills.

An officer of my equivalent rank was detailed to pick me up from the station. He briefed me about rations and other daily necessities required for the family. When we reached the house, packaged ration items had been stocked and there was enough to cater to our needs for a week. For the first time in my service life, I was warmly welcomed, briefed and looked after. It was a great *feel-good* factor.

The first few days

During the first few days, I familiarised myself with the surroundings as there were no classes. On one such occasion, I met an officer whom I asked for directions to the bakery. As we were walking towards the bakery, he told me that a lady officer was joining the course and he was very upset. He told me that till then, no lady service officer had attended the course. Neither did he ask me why I was there, nor did I volunteer to inform him. He possibly took me to be the wife of one of the newly posted *Directing Staff* (DS). When the classes started, he was my first DS and it was a sight to see his face when he saw me in uniform sitting in the very first row.

Meeting Field Marshal Manekshaw

On our first day in college, lunch was laid out in the officer's mess for all the student officers and the staff at DSSC. The Field Marshal was specially invited to meet all of us as he was living in Ooty at that time As I was the only Lady officer, he spoke to me first for few minutes and later went to meet the other student officers. After this personal interaction, I saw a huge portrait of Field Marshal Manekshaw in the mess ante-room. I kept looking at the painting and at him, but could not decipher who he was. Every other officer went and paid their respects and spoke to him. Finally, the mystery was too much for me and I asked one of my colleagues who he was. He was kind enough to tell me that he was Field Marshal Manekshaw. At the same time, he wondered how I did not recognise him. I felt very small. At the same time, I felt very proud to have interacted with Field Marshal Manekshaw. In fact, he appreciated and praised me since I was the first lady officer at DSSC.

A great learning experience

DSSC is a wonderful place and provided for a great learning experience. All the three services had their own classes under their respective wings. I was in the Air Wing. We also had combined classes with all the three wings, i.e. Army, Navy and Air Force. In addition, we had guest lectures by renowned scholars in various fields, the three service chiefs, ambassadors of other countries and many eminent people.

Officers...lady and officers

My first commandant was General Sethna. The usual address during classes was, "Good morning Officers". Now I was there. He was slightly confused in the initial stages. Sometimes he would say "lady officer and gentlemen officers", sometimes "lady and officers" and sometimes he would just forget to address us. One day, I requested him to continue addressing us, as officers and not to worry about addressing me as a special case. He was rather relieved and from then on it was 'officers'. The commandant was very worried because of my presence in DSSC. One day, he asked me whether I would create problems for him or the administration. I asked him what sort of problems. With a lot of hesitation, he confided that if I got pregnant or had an abortion, he wondered what would happen. At this, I almost burst out laughing. But, realising the gravity of the situation, I replied that I was a doctor and could look after myself, so he needn't worry on my account. His anxiety was thanks to a bad experience with a civilian lady officer during one of the previous courses. She had to be sent back. After this interaction, he was relieved. I not only took care of myself and my family as a doctor but also attended to all the medical issues of my colleagues and their families as a medical officer.

Every week, there was a get together at the commandant's residence for a group of foreign officers. This was aimed at making them comfortable and helping them get to know about India. I was a constant invitee for these parties at the commandant's house. It was a great experience to meet colleagues representing various countries, talking to them broadened my views and they also gained by interacting with me.

Locker number

At DSSC, "we student officers" were allotted a locker and the locker number was our identity. We had to submit assignments, some within a few hours and some within 24 hours. The time varied as per the toughness of the assignment. Once completed, you placed it in the DS's locker. During the first few days, I used to bring my work home. When I returned home, our younger son who was two years old then, would have come back from his nursery school and would be eating lunch. He would run to greet me, his hands full of rice and cooked lentil, and would hug me. His affection was delightful and I did not have the heart to stop him. But it led to one problem. My paper, which had to be completed and submitted, would have a rainbow of colours thanks to my son, Ajit. At DSSC, there were rules on how to write, label, tag and submit the papers. Corrections were made with red ink. Since my papers were a mess, there would be comments in red all over the sheets. My solution was to stay back at college, complete the work and deposit it in the DS's locker. After submission, I returned home. I did not have the heart to tell my child not to hug me. Now I was free to play with him and enjoy life.

Meeting my classmate

The course at DSSC was not tough but it was something new and I had to put in the extra effort. The joint exercises were fun. There used to be day and night exercises too. All this was not an issue for me as I was accustomed with night duties and call duties during my service life. Here, I met my AFMC classmate through her husband. While on a joint project, he told me that his wife too is a doctor from AFMC. Instantly, I realized she was my friend and told him so. We had a good time after that with lots of get-togethers and picnics. Her sons and my sons became great friends.

Recognition for MSc (Defence Sciences)

Madras University recognised the course and on successful completion of DSSC course, the officers would be awarded Master of Science (MSc) Defence Sciences degree. We had to pass all the weekly tests and submit a thesis to be approved by

Madras University to be eligible for the MSc degree. All my colleagues opted for Air Force topics and some for management topics. I chose the unique topic of the "Space Shuttle", which at that time was only in the drawing board stage. I had to study a lot and write up my thesis, which was appreciated by one and all. I was one amongst few who was awarded the MSc degree in Defence Studies. After completion of the course, we were also awarded the degree of "passed staff college" (psc) by the services. We could use this decoration with our name. When I went up on stage to collect my degree, the applause echoed in the auditorium for a long time, was a testimony to how much my teachers, colleagues and friends loved and respected me. I can still hear the clapping....

Forward area tour

There were some awkward moments during the course too. There was a field area tour both in the Eastern and Western sectors. I was not allowed to take part because I was the only lady officer. I told the authorities that I had no problem in participating, but they would not budge from their stand. In retrospect, I think they were correct. They wanted me to apply for annual leave and stay at home. I refused to do so as I was willing to go and they were not taking me. Finally, it was agreed that I would attend the college regularly, till the field area tour was over and that I need not apply for annual leave. Though I saved my annual leave, I missed the field area tour. Thus, I completed the DSSC course successfully with a 'passed staff college (psc)' and MSc, the second post-graduate degree to add to my kitty.

Extra-curricular activities

Along with the defence studies, there was a lot of scope for learning and a plethora of activities to choose from for lady wives. There was *batik, macramé,* painting, baking classes and games such as badminton, tennis, horse riding and more. With my feet in two different boats, one being the house and the second the college, I hardly found time to indulge in these activities. But, I did learn a few things: *batik fabric painting, macramé and candle making*. I also improved my game of badminton. It was a great place to learn new crafts. Sadly, for me, time was the limiting factor.

I spent most of my free time in the library. It was a four-storied building with plenty of books on a variety of subjects. My colleagues used to wonder why I was studying so hard. Truth be told, I wasn't really studying! I used to copy designs for knitting, embroidery, macramé, etc. from the basement of the library section. My mother and I, together knitted 26 pullovers during that one year. There was a sweater I knitted for my younger son, which was multicoloured, depicting the colours of the three services; it had a ship (the blue colour of the Navy) in the lowest panel, a tank (red, the colour of the Army) in the middle panel and an aircraft (in a grey-blue shade, the colour of the Air Force) in the top panel. The sweater was a huge hit in the Staff College. In a lighter vein, I think I was showered with more accolades for the sweater than for my successful completion of DSSC!

Queuing up for rations

Another awkward experience was collecting ration from the ration stand. Each service had their own peculiarities. Though the Army Wing had prohibited *batmen* (helpers) officially, all the army officers somehow managed to get batmen who would help the officers and their families. The Air Force does not have a system of batmen. I used to collect the rations for my family. I used to stand in a queue along with the batmen, who used to represent the officers. There was nothing I could do. We would stand in the queue, waiting for our turn. One particular officer's wife would walk into the ration stand and comment, "Darling, the ration is not even fit for dogs. Let us go and buy from outside." After a few days of listening to such comments, one day I exploded at the officer. I told him not to come to the ration stand and that if he came, he should ensure that his wife behaved properly. I was his senior. He had to tolerate my outburst. He left the ration stand in a huff with his darling wife. Thankfully, they never came back to the ration stand.

Golf set

The Canteen Stores Department (CSD) canteen used to offer items for sale like a half golf set or six foreign whiskies. You could buy either one of them. I chose the golf set, dreaming of playing golf. But I never did! Even in later service life, we never found time to play golf. My husband was instrumental in the construction of the golf course at Hebbal, Training Command. But not a single day did we play. The job, family, higher education for ourselves, education of the children and other numerous commitments ate up all our time and today, I just stare at the old golf set! I wonder at times whether it would have been better if we had learned golf. At the end of the day, those for whom you have toiled so hard leave you for their call of duty. They may not even realize your sacrifices. The lifeless golf set stares at me every day, making me reminisce about those days. When I pass the golf course at Noida, I still have a strong sense of guilt at not having picked up the game. The beauty of golf is that you can play it if you want to even up to a ripe old age. You can play as much as you want or as little as you choose. You inhale pure fresh air at the golf course, meet your friends and spend time happily. By the time our commitments were over, and we did have the time to play golf, we were not physically fit or mentally inclined due to old age. But I still miss not playing golf. It's a great game which, sadly, I never got down to learning.

People's taunts

As I was the first lady doing the course, my poor husband had to endure several taunts. At every party or get-together, the first question shot at him was why had he not been selected for DSSC. He answered this question umpteen times and finally gave up. He stopped attending those functions. I used to feel equally miserable at the direct and indirect taunts which followed us. We both were Air Force officers and almost everyone there knew about us. It is a small world. People take rather too much interest in your life but not as well-wishers. They want to make your life miserable and enjoy the devilish fun that they derive from that.

This put a lot of stress on both of us. To overcome the stress and to prevent a mental breakdown, I adopted a novel method. I started writing 'Om Sai Ram' every day. This gave me the moral courage to tell others to shut up and mind their own business. To date, I continue this ritual. I must confess that taking Lord Almighty's name gives you the moral strength to face any crisis.

My parents' support

My parents were living with us as my husband was posted in a different unit. They looked after the house, the children and me as I was busy with my studies. My mother used to look after the kitchen and knit sweaters for all of us during her free time. My father used to take the children to school, buy vegetables and fruits, etc. and play tennis in the evenings. He was an excellent tennis player at DSSC. My father used to fast for the entire day on Thursday, Saturdays, *Amavasya* (new moon day) and numerous religious festivals. At present, he is hundred years old, fit and fine and walks erect.

Rudrakshas and films

I remember our house was very close to the famous Sim's Park in Coonoor. The boys and their friends used to love the park and would visit it often. There is a huge *Rudraksha* tree in the park, one of the few of these rare trees whose seeds are considered auspicious. The kids would slide down the hilly path and search for *Rudrakshas* all around the tree and at the base of the tree. They used to dig the soil with their tiny hands to find *rudrakshas* and would then come running to tell me how many *rudrakshas* they had collected. My father made a necklace with the rudrakshas they collected and donated it to the Lord Vinayaka temple.

The children enjoyed their stay at DSSC. Every week, two films were screened - one in English and another in an Indian language. They would watch the films without fail, whether they understood them or not. They had to carry their passes and be on time. If you were late and the doors had closed, they would not be opened for anyone.

Miraculous escapes

Once my husband and I were going somewhere in a one-tonner in Ooty. Driving along winding, hilly roads, we both were seated in front with the army driver at the steering wheel; my husband was in the middle and I was next to the door. Maybe I had not closed the door properly. Suddenly, the door flung open. I was not holding on to anything and I started to fall out. My husband had the presence of mind to hold on to my legs and feet and called out to stop the vehicle at once. It was like a scene from a Bollywood film except that it was real life. I was hanging upside down for some time and was rescued by the driver and other passers-by. My husband held on to my legs and feet till help arrived.

I recall another incident too. Whenever I think about it or talk about it, I develop goose pimples. My husband was posted in Coimbatore, which is in the foothills of Ooty. He used to come up once in two weeks and I used to go down once in two weeks. On one Saturday, I had gone with the kids to Coimbatore as usual. I always used to return on Sunday evening.

When I had gone down that weekend, the ensuing Monday, I was the team leader for the whole class and we had to do a presentation. On that Sunday, in my husband's unit, there was a farewell party for a brother officer. He asked me to stay back for the party and told me that I could take the first bus from Coimbatore at 4 am to reach college on time. I agreed. The next morning, the three of us boarded the bus at 4 am. The journey was uneventful till Mettupalayam. And then, suddenly, the driver and the passengers realized that the road had been barricaded with big boulders and there was a huge crowd swarming across the road. The driver stopped and asked us to get off the vehicle at once. There was a farmer's agitation going on. We did not know about it. Luckily, the bus stopped next to the railway station and a train was waiting to leave for Ooty. Our elder son carried the bags and I carried the sleeping baby (who was around two-and-half years old). The crowd pelted stones at us. My children and I were injured in the stone pelting and we were bleeding. Somehow, we boarded the train and reached Coonoor railway station. Now, we faced another problem - how were we to reach DSSC? There were no vehicles and no taxis. There was no way I could have walked with two children and the luggage. Fortunately for us, a gentleman on a motorbike approached me. He told me that he was a Havildar or Subedar from MES, I do not remember now. He offered to drop us home. Usually, I never take a lift from anyone. Under dire situations and as a last resort, I may take a lift from a *Fauji*. This gentleman not only knew about me but also described our house, the fittings, the macramé, the paintings, etc. I was totally convinced that he was an army personnel from MES. He also confirmed that he had visited our house many times for various repair works. I accepted his offer and got onto his bike along with the children, and we reached home safely. When I left for Coimbatore, my parents had also left to attend some social function. No one was at home. I left the children bleeding and hungry under the care of God Almighty. I quickly changed into uniform, reported to DSSC on time and completed my presentation. It went off very well. I came back home, cooked for the kids and after feeding them, took them to the hospital to get their wounds cleaned and for first aid treatment.

After all, this was done, I went to the Military Engineering Service (MES) office to thank my saviour. I enquired high and low and discovered that there was no such person in that MES office. WHO WAS HE? I still do not know the answer. But, I know one thing, if you call God Almighty for help with sincere prayers, 'He' will come to help you. If I had not reached the college on time, I could have been court-martialed as I had not taken prior permission to stay out of DSSC on Sunday night. It was my first experience of the Almighty in physical form. My husband came to know about the strike in the evening when he read the newspapers. He called me up on the Officer's Mess telephone; it was only then that I burst out crying. I told him about the entire incident. He was, naturally, relieved when he heard my voice and knew that the children and I had reached safely.

Thus, I completed the DSSC course successfully and was posted out to a field area in the Western sector. My husband's posting followed soon after. We had wanted to be posted together after DSSC and that dream was achieved but at a tremendous price.

Scientific Experiments in the Icy Arctic

I was posted at Defence Institute of Physiology and Allied Sciences (DIPAS) from Bangalore. During that period, DIPAS undertook an international project along with the then Union of Soviet Socialist Republic (USSR). This Indo Soviet project (HIMDOM) was conceived, planned and executed to study the effects of extreme cold on tropical Indian soldiers. Further, the project aimed to find out if *acclimatisation* was possible in an extremely cold environment. I must explain the significance of the name 'HIMDOM'- '*HIM*' in Sanskrit means ice or snow and '*DOMA*' in Russian stands for a house or dwelling. Thus, the icy Arctic was to be our home for nearly four months during the extreme winter months from November 1989 to February 1990.

Travelling to Moscow

Dr W Selvamurthy was our team leader while I was the doctor, physiologist and *2i/c* of the team. Along with us, scientists from DIPAS and ten physically fit soldiers, selected from all the four corners of India, comprised the Indian team. The team leader, along with four Indian scientists, left in the advance party. One scientist, I and ten soldiers along with the equipment were airlifted in November 1989 to Moscow. The flight was very comfortable and the International Airport at Moscow was warm and cozy. Later, we headed to the domestic airport. It was a complete contrast to the International Airport; there was no heating and the cold was freezing our bones. We had left Delhi early in the morning and by the time we arrived at the domestic airport, it was noon and we were very hungry. There was no money, i.e. *roubles* with us. A guide from the Russian Embassy who was proficient in English was to help us in arranging our dinner and boarding the train to Murmansk. We waited patiently, very patiently, very patiently for the guide but there was no sign of him. It was late evening and we'd still not had any food, not even a cup of tea. One could buy cigarettes but there were no tea or coffee stalls. We were cursing our luck. At last, Mr. Alexander, our guide proficient in English, arrived. He hardly knew any English. Anyway, he ordered food for all of us which was totally non-vegetarian. There was no concept of vegetarian food. I had already been briefed about the food problem. So, I had carried *avakkai* pickle (mango pickle) made by my mother. I was eagerly awaiting *roti* and finally, *Khlep (bread)* arrived on the scene. All of us literally attacked our food and gobbled it down; we were starving! The first Russian words, I learnt were *khlep* and *niyat masa* for my survival in this alien land.

A train journey to remember

We travelled from Moscow to Murmansk by train. Murmansk is in the Arctic Circle near Barent sea and the Arctic ocean (Latitude - 68°58' and Longitude - 33° 5'). Russians do not seem to be travel bugs like Indians. There were very few Russians on the train; we Indians seemed to outnumber them. As a result, we spent the journey playing a*ntakshari*. We were all singing quite loudly and almost the whole train was entertained. We chose all the old Hindi songs from Raj Kapoor's films, which are evergreen melodies and hot favourites of the Russians. At the end of the journey, many co-passengers gifted us whatever they had. The most common gift was tinned tuna fish, which is a delicacy in Russia. My colleagues enjoyed the same. I was the only fish out of water. One tin was kept aside for me, the lead singer, to take home to my family. What surprised me were the gifts. At that time, the USSR was going through *Perestroika* meaning restructuring under their leader, Mikhail Gorbachev. Despite their own difficulties, they were generous enough, to give up their favourite food for us. Most often, the gifts that we received were common day-to-day utility items.

One striking feature of Russian stations was that there were no food stalls or hawkers on the platforms selling foodstuff – something so commonplace in India. The platforms were practically empty and scrupulously clean. The journey was not very long. The railways provide bedding and free tea (any amount you could consume). The TTE was a lady (a little more than plump) and she served us tea (without milk) from a massive *samovar*. In Russian, *samovar* means a heated metal container, traditionally used to heat and boil water. A similar vessel is also used in Kashmir. The heated water was used to make tea whenever we asked for some. Traveling by train in the USSR was most certainly an interesting experience. From Murmansk, we travelled to our destination (close to Barent sea) in the icy Arctic by road in large vehicles running with snow chains or tire chains. These are devices fitted to the tyres of the vehicles to provide maximum traction when driving through snow and ice. Snow chains attach to the drive wheels of a vehicle.

Life in the icy Arctic

We unpacked the equipment and set up our laboratory, which took us approximately a week. The USSR team consisted of scientists from the fields of biochemistry, psychology and electrophysiology. Thirty Russian soldiers were also part of the study. I was the only lady and medical doctor in the team.

Our day started at 4:30 am (local time) with yoga and exercise. The temperature would normally hover around -30° C to -35° C. When the winds howled, the temperature dropped to -45° C due to the *wind chill factor*. There was no sun or sunlight throughout our stay because these were winter months (polar nights of continuous three months from November to January). The Arctic and the extreme northern hemisphere have long winters and long summers (six months). In addition, magnetic forces are high at the poles and this results in deleterious health effects if exposed for a long time. As our stay was of a short duration, we did not suffer any long-term health effects. The few locals who were employed in mines and other activities suffered many lifestyle disorders such as hypertension and lung diseases, to quote a few. The people who worked there were transferred to Moscow or better locales when they reached around forty years of age. They were also provided with a house by the Government as an incentive at that time.

Scientific studies

The aim of our project was to find answers to the following questions: Whether tropical Indians can acclimatise to the extreme cold? If they could, how long (duration) would it take them to acclimatise? If acclimatised, what are the changes taking place physiologically, biochemically, electrophysiologically and psychologically, which lead to the acclimatisation? Are these changes temporary or permanent in nature? What will be the food requirements during this phase of acclimatisation? Would they require any special or additional food supplies? What essential clothing (especially for the extremities) were needed in extremely cold conditions? And when the tropical Indian returned to India, how long would these changes last?

Why was it important to know the answers to these questions? In modern-day warfare, the soldier moves to various places with extreme climates. In that scenario, is he able to cope or not and if he does, how long would it take him to reach his full capability. Does he need special food or clothing to improve his capabilities? These were the riddles to be solved. Why in the icy Arctic? In India, the places which are extremely cold are at altitudes and not on plains. The high altitude adds another dimension of hypoxic stress along with cold stress. The aim was to study the effects of extreme cold. One may postulate that modern-day warfare is extremely tech-savvy. Indeed so. But, finally, it is the foot soldier who holds the land after victory. The above project was to understand the difficulties, if any, and to ameliorate them as much as possible so that the foot soldier can perform at his optimum best.

Initially, the physical, physiological, biochemical, psychological and electrophysiological parameters of all the Indian soldiers were recorded in Delhi, and this served as the baseline reading. Soon after their arrival, the same parameters were recorded, both by Indian and Russian scientists, on both

Indian and Russian soldiers. This was to find out the changes in Indian soldiers from what had been observed in Delhi and also to compare their values with those of Russian soldiers.

After a period of nine to ten days, wherein they were exposed to harsh environmental conditions and standard physical exercises as carried out in the army during peacetime, the same parameters were recorded again. Subsequently, every nine to ten days the parameters were recorded. After the initial deterioration, the values improved steadily and reached their baseline value between four to five weeks of exposure to cold. By the end of six weeks, almost all of them had reached their baseline values and some achieved even better results. This was the hallmark that the Indian soldiers had acclimatised to the extreme cold. Further studies did not show any significant changes. This stage of acclimatisation was lost after ten days of returning back to Delhi, India thus confirming that it was temporary and not permanent.

What did we find out from this research? We found that Indians could acclimatise to extreme cold over a period of about four to six weeks and this lasted till we came back to India. Gradually, the acclimatisation was lost over a span of ten to fifteen days. The special multi-layered clothing, including gloves and shoes, were designed and improvised locally to overcome the effects of extreme cold. One of the unexpected findings was that a soldier from the hot and humid state of Kerala withstood the effects of extreme cold the best, better than the soldiers hailing from the hills or from North India. As we could not find any answer to this phenomenon, we attributed it to *cross-acclimatisation*. I'm not very sure about this finding as the sample size was very small - just ten soldiers.

Administrative functions

As mentioned above, the Indian team's schedule started at 4:30 am (local time) with yoga and exercise. Two officers and three sepoys formed one group and there were three such groups - one group for road management, one for food (warming the readymade food prepared by a Defence Food Research Laboratory (DFRL) in Mysore) and fetching ice for drinking water and the third one for cleaning the toilets (pit latrines). These duties were rotated every week. Each one of us was part of these teams with no exceptions.

The road management team removed the piled-up snow every two hours, or in even less time, depending on the quantum of snowfall. If the snow was not removed, the roads would get blocked. The roads were cleaned with huge wooden brooms. The job involved physical labour as there were no motorized vehicles to remove the ice. It was extremely tiring.

The food team chalked out the menu as per the availability of rations. They warmed the food packets we had carried from the food lab at Mysuru. One great advantage was the availability of plenty of live fish below the frozen snow. Our team members used to break the frozen snow, catch the live fish and cook simple but delicious dishes. The cooking and warming of food was done using kerosene stoves. On the very first day, a huge quantity of bread was supplied; it was meant to last us for the entire four months. One of us commented that it would go bad. But, corrected ourselves instantaneously, realising that we were living at temperatures of -45° C. I was the one who had a tough time as I was a pure vegetarian. I survived on bread and the pickles that I had carried from home. There was one silver lining: either buttermilk or fruit juice used to be supplied once a week, especially for me. The rest were quite jealous!

The Russian bath

For six days of the week, we worked hard day and night as per the schedule of experiments. A lot of the equipment used to go bad or not work satisfactorily due to the extreme cold. We became experts at fixing them. Sunday was a holiday, the day to have a Russian bath and to communicate with family members. The Russian bath or *Banya* in Russian is a small room where you are exposed to dry or wet heat sessions. You perspire after this, wipe yourself dry and you are supposed to have bathed. Something akin to a modern *sauna bath*. I was not a part of this bath.

Communication

We were provided with a telephone system. (I have forgotten what it was called). Family members assembled at Army Headquarters, New Delhi at a fixed time on Sunday morning. Each one of us could speak with our family members for 10 minutes. It was something like a walkie-talkie. First, you would speak while they listened; when they spoke at the other end, you listened. This was the only umbilical cord with our families in India. We used to await Sundays to speak to our dear ones eagerly.

The medical doctor's role

I was detailed to visit a nearby mining area twice a week to examine, investigate and treat the local population working there in addition to my research duties. During the process of my interaction with the patients and hospital staff, I picked up a few Russian words. Most of the local populace had lung problems due to their work in the deep mines and the pollution thereof. I had carried some medicines with me which I distributed. Later, they bought the medicines themselves. As mentioned earlier, this was the time of *Perestroika*. It was a tough time for the common man because of the transitions that were taking place. On the days of hospital duty, I was picked up in a car from our research laboratory and taken to the hospital and dropped back. I must confess that I had my bath at the hospital twice a week.

It was a wonderful experience to work in the hospital and help patients. They were also very happy with me. After the four months, on the last day of my hospital duty, there was a lengthy farewell speech which I did not understand. The head of the hospital presented me *gift hamper* containing liquor bottles. I preserved it carefully and my family enjoyed the high-quality liquor when I returned to India.

A magnificent sight

One day, as I was returning late in the evening after attending to patients, the driver suddenly stopped the car. He was very excited and rattled off something in Russian. I did not understand and was scared; I thought that my end was near as I was alone in the snowbound Arctic far away from my near and dear ones. He signalled me to get out of the car and pointed at the sky. What a wonderful sight! I was so lucky to witness it. The sky was lit up in a rainbow of electrifying colours - green, blue, yellow, orange... all swiftly changing. I have no words to describe this visual treat. I had no camera with me to take photos. There were no 2G, 3G or 4G cell phones in 1989. But, it was a lifetime experience. The rest of the team members were so jealous because I was the only one to witness the magnificent panorama of Aurora Borealis. *Aurora Borealis* or Northern Lights are seen in clear skies at high latitudes in the Arctic. It can also be seen in countries located in extreme latitudes in the Northern hemisphere. This phenomenon can also be witnessed in the Southern polar regions and extreme latitudes and is known as Aurora Australis. It is believed that solar winds react with the high magnetic fields in the polar regions, resulting in the magnificent light display.

Calling for a toast

Whenever we visited someone in their homes or at the laboratory or when guests came calling on us at the campsite, they used to raise a toast to their nations. I had never been a part of a toasting ceremony till then because I was a junior officer. Here, in the Arctic, I was second in seniority, so I had to raise the toast many times. Vodka was always available, but I was a teetotaler. I was scared of drinking hard liquor because I feared that I might lose my cool in front of the soldiers. You can call it officer's pride. To avoid drinking vodka, I kept a glass of water next to me. Luckily for me, the colour of vodka was the same as water. As soon as the toast was over, I would change the glass in a jiffy and drink water to my heart's content. My colleagues had their suspicions as to what I was drinking. Much later, when we were back in Delhi, I revealed the truth.

Visiting Leningrad, Moscow and Kiev

After completing our scientific work, we left our campsite. We had a break of seven days which we spent sightseeing in Leningrad (St Petersburg), Moskva (Moscow) and Kiev. The Winter Palace at Leningrad is exquisitely beautiful. There are no words to describe the beauty of the paintings and other artefacts. What impressed me most was the way they cared about their history and culture. The guide would not allow us to go near the paintings and statues, leave alone touch them. One of the soldiers tried to touch something. He was immediately thrown out of the museum. Their strict discipline and our behaviour are diametrically opposite. It is a common sight in India to see vulgar inscriptions and the disfigurement of paintings and sculptures at our heritage sites. What a sad contrast!

Shopping in Russia

During this well-deserved break, we had some memorable shopping experiences. There were huge multi-storied malls with many shops; there were no items to buy! The shelves were practically empty. I compared the malls to our shops in India. Even the smallest shop in Karol Bagh in New Delhi had more items and different varieties of goods for sale. These shops were like our ration shops. Every item required by the local people was issued against something like a ration card, which the individual had to produce in order to shop. Even mink coats were available on ration cards once in two-three years. The catch was that they could only buy from their allotted shops. They could not go to another shop if the size or colour was not available in their allotted shop. On any day, clothes were available in one colour and one size only. I presumed that they came in lots every few weeks. The shoppers had no choice except to pick up what was available, even if it was not the colour of their choice or their size. The simplest solution was to alter the clothing to fit to the person's size and to accept the colour displayed in the store if one needed it badly. Otherwise, one had to wait till one's choice comes up for sale. The woollen items were very good but there was not much choice in cotton items. We bought a few items as souvenirs. Bills were made for us as a special case. The bill was totalled on an *abacus* and not on an electronic calculator. It sure looked primitive!

All in all, it was a wonderful experience. We succeeded in our scientific experiments. We also learnt to live and work as a team, bonding and sharing one another's happy and sad moments, far away from our families. We kept the Indian flag flying high with our scientific knowledge and our social interactions.

After sightseeing and shopping, we returned to Delhi. I was wearing two woollen coats, (which I had bought in Russia), one over the other, and looked like a clown. One important unofficial result of our Arctic expedition was that all of us had turned fairer by at least three to four shades, as depicted in the 'Fair and Lovely' advertisement. There was no 'sunlight' in the Arctic region, to tan us.

In Tamil, there is a saying, "Thirai kadal oodium, dravyam thedu", I crossed many countries and reached the icy Arctic. I did not get wealth but the name and fame which followed me were phenomenal. I was the first Indian lady to step into the subzero Arctic.

Jai Hind!

Gender - A Blessing or a Curse?

Aavadum Pennale, Azhivadum Pennale (Tamil) means that 'all that is created is by women and all that is destroyed is also by women'.

Yatra naryaha Pujyante, tatra ramante Devaha. (Sanskrit) translates as – 'where women are worshipped the angels come there'.

Historical perspective

In India, women were held in high esteem in our scriptures and during the Vedic period. Medieval India saw the steep decline in women's status. During this period, privileges and discrimination were not only caste-based but also gender-based. Killing a woman was a comparatively lighter offence, like drinking alcohol. The sole aim of a woman was to give birth to male progeny. In 'Padma Purana', Sage Vasishta ordained women to obey menfolk throughout life. Even in Tulsidasji's 'Ram Charit Manas', women are equated to Shudras, the lowest in the caste hierarchy and *pashu*, the animal. Sati, the practice of a widow self-immolating on her husband's pyre, was in practice till not very long ago. The present-day picture too is not very rosy.

What is the status of women in the so-called advanced western culture? How many of us are aware that their womenfolk went through similar prejudices till about two or three hundred years back? The most advanced country in terms of political freedom in Europe is France. But, France did not give voting rights to women for a very long time. Women were clubbed with minors, the poor and landless labourers who too did not have voting rights. Throughout Europe, the dress code for aristocratic women was strict. They had to wear uncomfortable dresses to highlight their physical beauty. The Industrial Revolution brought in machines which helped women to undertake many activities hitherto reserved only for men. It was not because of any magic; the machines needed less of brawn and maybe more of brains. The world wars too resulted in acute shortage of manpower for war activities. Thus, women gained some economic freedom by working in factories and aiding in war efforts, especially during the second world war. In many western countries, political participation in the form of voting rights for women came up only during the second half of the 20th century.

I am trying to collate my experiences on gender equality or discrimination as I perceived it. During my childhood and adolescence, I never knew about this word as the treatment given was accepted as the norm b the majority of women. Maybe few protested or raised their voice, but that went unheeded. I believed in the same social fabric. Over time, when I comprehended the discrimination, I desisted from confronting the issues headlong. I tried to overcome them by adapting to the situation.

My maternal grandfather

When I look back at my grandfather's behaviour, I wonder whether it was gender discrimination. In an earlier chapter, I had talked about how, if by any chance the food was delayed, my grandfather used to throw the cutting board (*aruvamanai*) at my grandmother. And how, when we used to visit them during the holidays, he would make special *dosai* for my elder brother but would never give me even a small bit. He was very short tempered and did not believe in gender equality.

The obsession with having a son

Remember the story of my mother's paternal aunt - *Chitti,* who adopted a son as they did not have any children? In one of my previous chapters, I have described her plight in detail. My grandfather had vehemently opposed the decision to adopt a son, but my *Chitti* had been determined. Why? Because in India, we are obsessed with the concept of having sons.

My PT teacher

My Physical training (PT) teacher, was one of the two north Indians in our school. He understood a bit of Tamil and managed well, unlike my Hindi teacher, Shri Aryaji. My elder brother was his pet student. I had never played any game, but I had watched my father playing tennis and my elder brother playing almost all games at school. Unlike other girls in my class, I expressed a desire to play ring tennis to the PT teacher. He made a caustic remark saying that girls do not play and if I wanted to play I should play *langri tang*. So, I asked him for *chuna* powder to mark the boundaries on the ground for *langri tang*. To this, he said, "Pick up the dry leaves and use them to mark the boundary." I did feel bad at that time, but it was not a big deal because girls did not play games in those days. Was this gender bias? Was it the accepted norm? No one had coined the phrase Gender Discrimination then. Look at today, PV Sindhu, Saina Nehwal, Sania Mirza, Mary Kom, Phogat sisters, to name a few are creating history in the world of sports.

Later, an opportunity did come my way, but I failed miserably. At that time, the Health Minister was Rajkumari Amrit Kaur, if my memory is correct. She had started coaching classes for girls from Delhi schools for all games. Girls from my school were to be coached in hockey. For the first time in my life, I wore a divided skirt as that was the prescribed uniform. I was very self-conscious about my outfit and concentrated more on it than on the hockey stick or the hockey ball. I was pulling down my skirt all the time. Remember the scene in 'Dangal' movie where the young ladies are pulling down their skirts, when they wore skirts for the first time. The other girls thrashed me with their hockey sticks. That was the first and last day of my participation in sports activities in the school.

Higher secondary education in the Humanities stream

I did well in class VIII and was offered the science group, which was also my choice. But my mother was against it. She was told that students sustain burn injuries while conducting chemistry practicals. Her chief concern was my marriage; "who would marry me if I sustain burn injuries"! The second reason was the science stream was only available at the Lodi Road school, which was quite far from our house. She did not want me to travel by public transport since I was approaching my menarche. But, I was never informed about any of this. There was no sex education in those days. There was a financial angle too. If I took up humanities, I could use the old tattered books that my cousins had used earlier, so new books needn't be bought. Finally, it was decided that I would study humanities at Gole Market school.

Amma in her own clever way made me a student of domestic science which had almost the same curriculum as that of modern day *Home Science*. Well, I did not pursue it for long. In those days and even today in many places in India, girls do not plan their futures; their parents decide it for them. Girls did not study for the love of a subject, as a career option or for passion. They just went to school or college till an ideal groom was arranged, a groom who fulfilled the QRs set by the family. In many houses, girls were never sent to school and if they did go to school, their student life came to an end, when they attained *menarche*. That was the social norm. Is it discrimination? I do not know.

When a daughter wants to pursue something outside the established norms, all hell will break loose, whereas a son is always encouraged. Why these double standards? Is it gender discrimination? I do not know.

Internship trying to learn ECG

By now I had qualified in MBBS with flying colours and was undergoing compulsory internship. Electrocardiography (ECG) was carried out in speciality hospitals and that too under the direct supervision of medical specialists. The Medical Specialist would take out the ECG machine from a locked cupboard and after recording the ECG, would put the machine back in the cupboard and lock it again. I was dying to learn the technique and the interpretation of ECG. I had learnt everything about ECG and the great scientist Einthoven, to impress my teachers. But, all my efforts were in vain. The Professor, Medical Specialist and others in the department would always tell me to go to the gynaecology department. The male interns used to surround the patient and the machine. I used to climb on a chair to see what was going on. If any of the seniors spotted me, they would shout at me and tell me to go to the gynaecology department. Mind you, these people were highly educated, progressive-minded service doctors. Was it gender discrimination? I wonder.

Dreams of motherhood

Every woman dreams of motherhood. The ladies who attended the antenatal clinic were either wives of officers or the air warriors and their equivalents in the other two services. For local officer's wives, it was a time to meet their friends and exchange notes in the hospital. In addition, they attended to banking jobs, buying groceries, visiting the CSD canteen to buy the latest arrivals and, if time permitted, they would visit the central school nearby to find out the progress of their wards, if any. All this was possible because the hospital, MI room, banks, canteen and schools were located in the non-technical or domestic area.

Thursday was *antenatal* day. The *primipara's* would be decked up in their finery and best jewellery when they reported for their antenatal check-up. If the husband accompanied the wife, he would dote on her. If he was at work, the in-laws used to accompany the lady and she would be pampered during the hospital visit. They would all be sitting, eating and gossiping amongst themselves.

When their turn came, the pregnant ladies would enter with an elaborate '*Sat Sri Akal*' and sit down. When you asked them their history, if it were their first pregnancy, they would be very shy and it was a tough job to extract answers. If they had a few children, they would count the boys as their children and leave out the girls. And, if they had only girls, when asked how many children they had, they would say none. The girl child was not counted as a child. If they had two or three daughters and no son, they would cry inconsolably. After consoling them and making them comfortable, when you asked them why they had cried, they would detail the torture they faced at home. The poor daughters too were not spared. They hardly got anything to eat, leave alone a balanced diet. Punjab was the land of plenty but the fair sex had to put up with a lot of hardship. These incidents I am recounting happened in the early 70s. We can see the result today, in the form of the skewed sex ratio all over India; but it is much worse in Punjab and Haryana (undivided Punjab then).

Those were the days of no ultrasonography and hence there was no sex determination possible. The people had tremendous belief that the doctor would be able to detect the sex of the *foetus*. They also believed that if the doctor had a son and if you were treated by that doctor, you too would have a son. If you lived in a rented house and the owner had sons, you too would have a son. These superstitions were fed into the minds of the pregnant lady by their relatives. They were looked after well during their first pregnancy. If it was a second pregnancy after giving birth to a son, then the lady was treated like a queen. The doctor attending to her was also treated with a lot of love and respect and showered with gifts. On the other hand, if a woman's firstborn was a girl, everyone would have long faces and would pray for a son and not another daughter. If they had four or five daughters, the ladies underwent the rigours of repeated pregnancies in addition to tough household chores, in the hope of hitting the jackpot, i.e. giving birth to a son. This group almost always came trooping along with their daughters. For me, it was a learning curve: the impact of a patriarchal society and its gender preferences. I am quite certain there was no foeticide in those days since they did not know the sex of the baby before birth. However, I don't know if infanticide was practised.

My first flying experience

Around this time, a new fighter trainer (Iskara) had been introduced in the IAF and myself and another doctor were detailed to fly in the aircraft with the pilot to detect any man-machine mismatch (*human factors*). Both of us reported to the Air Force Academy (AFA) at Dindigul, Hyderabad. AOC, AFA Air Vice Marshal was very upset and was fuming when he learnt that a lady Aviation Medicine Specialist had been detailed to fly the aircraft both during day and night. He thundered and said women officers were not allowed to fly in fighter aircrafts. I was very frightened by his outburst, but gathered courage and fished out the orders for me to fly. When he realized that the orders were from his boss, he could not refuse me. An order is an order. I was reluctantly permitted to fly the newly-inducted jet trainer. Was this gender discrimination?

Thankfully, times have changed. Today, we have women fighter pilots in India. The IAF has really progressed to keep abreast with the changing times.

Selection for post-graduation

The theory exams were over. I had done exceedingly well in both surgery and medicine and was very happy that I would be recommended for MD General Medicine, my dream. When my turn came for viva voce, the professor intentionally asked me several questions about my parents, their health, my family, children and my cooking capabilities. Half an hour went by, I begged the professor to ask me at least one question in medicine. His answer was, I quote, "Go, go, look after your family and children. What will you do by doing MD Medicine?" And down came the curtains on my dream to become a medical specialist and cardiologist like Dr Padmavathy. I, Squadron Leader Padma Bandopadhyay (nee Dr S Padmavathy) became an Aviation Medicine specialist instead. Completing the course successfully, was a real testimony to *breaking the glass ceiling*. Today we have an equal number of men and women doctors in this speciality. The professor tried and succeeded in dashing my dreams, but unwittingly, he enabled me to become the first aviation medicine specialist in South-East Asia. Was it gender discrimination? I will leave it to you to decide.

Squadron Medical Officer (SMO)

I made it a point to visit and speak to the pilots and find out about any problems they might face. They used to confide in me about their family problems like wife's pregnancy, problems following abortions, children's issues and anything under the sun except aviation issues. It was difficult for them to accept me as one of them. They respected me but no way was I their squadron doctor. What could I do? After some soul-searching, I debated and discussed the issue with my friend, philosopher and guide, i.e. my husband. He advised me to take up training sorties in my squadron's trainer aircraft as and when possible. This trick worked. I flew as many sorties as possible. This made them realize that I was genuinely interested in their flying issues and gradually, they accepted me. You have to be a fighter boy to be considered one amongst them. Once the ice was broken between us, their problems came pouring down like an avalanche. It was frustrating when I had been unable to penetrate the, *my boy* syndrome. Later, when I became part and parcel of the squadron, I enjoyed my contribution, and they benefited from my advice. The initial cold shouldering was not because I lacked qualifications and experience, but because I was the first lady aviation specialist. Was it a gender bias? It took some time for them to understand and accept me.

Improving my medical qualifications

I had not yet acquired a postgraduate degree and both my age and seniority were going against me. I kept applying but got no replies. In government services and more so in the armed forces, the application goes through many official and unofficial channels. I was not selected even though, I was the most decorated soldier and had done well in all the service courses. Finally, after almost two years, I came to know that the services did not want to recommend me for General Medicine even though many of my friends were doing MD courses at the very same time. There were many official and unofficial considerations. There is a saying, "You show me the face, and I will quote the rule." The least they could have done to help me out was to be upfront and convey their decision. I lost two precious years waiting for their verdict. Due to various reasons, I was not considered fit to be a medical specialist. Maybe, I am not sure though, one of the reasons was that I was a lady.

SMO Madam

I was posted as the Senior Medical Officer (SMO) as well as Squadron Medical Officer. I had to interact with my boss at Headquarters. I requested the telephone operator to connect me to the Principal Medical Officer (PMO), my immediate boss. The air warrior was apprehensive on hearing a lady's voice. He repeatedly asked me why I wanted to speak to the PMO. My explanation that I was the SMO and I had to discuss some technical issues with PMO. This explanation fell on deaf ears. I devised a new method. I decided to pretend to be a secretary. I would tell the air warrior that 'Sir' wanted to speak to the PMO. They would connect my call in a jiffy. While I would be discussing some important issue, they would interrupt, asking, "Why are you speaking to PMO and not Sir? Let Sir come on the line." If I continued the discussion, they would disconnect the line. I understood it would take some time for them to get to know that their SMO happened to be a lady. Over time, the AF station got used to me and everyone got used to the SMO Madam. The station was used to lady doctors in uniform (LMO) but not a lady SMO.

My friend

I met this friend after many years. She had completed her graduation, married and was the mother of two young girls when I met her. I was so happy to meet her and wanted to spend time with her. But, she was passing through a very tough phase in her life at that time. Her husband had separated from her and was living with another lady. It was shocking and heartbreaking. The reason he'd left her was even more shocking: because she'd given birth to two daughters. Is it not absurd? Though, not giving birth to a son is a common reason for divorce in India. Today, both the young ladies are married and well settled in life and are a great support to their mother. What do you call this?

My service career

I have never faced sexual harassment during my years in the Air Force. All my colleagues and brother officers respected me and encouraged me. However, there was a lot of covert discrimination in the work arena. As a woman, you had to be three times more capable than your counterparts if you wanted to prove yourself.

Gender equality, gender mainstreaming and many such phrases are coined daily and are a dime a dozen. The preference for boys is a curse in Indian society and has assumed draconian proportions, leading to foeticide and infanticide, consequently resulting in a skewed sex ratio in India. Successive governments have been trying to frame rules and regulations and various schemes like the *Sukanya scheme* and *reservations* in educational institutions to name a few. These schemes aim to achieve or at least provide a better platform for girls and women. In my view, men must change their attitude and mindset towards the fair sex. The fair sex must also fight their own battles by studying hard, excelling in games and sports, following productive lifestyles and breaking the glass ceilings instead of waiting for the crumbs thrown at them occasionally.

I will conclude by saying:

"Beti Desh ki Jaan hai,
Beti Desh ki Shaan Hai
Isliye
Beti bachao,
Beti padao"

What is the actual status of women in India today?

A long way to go but the baby steps have already begun